PLANKING

GRILLING WITH PLANKS FOR UNBEATABLE BARBECUE FLAVOR

~SECRETS~

PLANKING

GRILLING WITH PLANKS FOR UNBEATABLE BARBECUE FLAVOR

SECRETS

Ron Shewchuk
www.RonShewchuk.com

whitecap

Edited by Elaine Jones
Proofread by Marial Shea and Ben D'Andrea
Cover and interior design by Jacqui Thomas
Food photographs by Greg Athans
Food styling by Nathan Fong
Additional photography by Ron Shewchuk and Bryan O'Connor

Visit Ron Shewchuk's website at www.ronshewchuk.com.

Printed and bound in Canada by Friesens

LIBRARY AND ARCHIVES CANADA CATALOGUING IN PUBLICATION
Shewchuk, Ron
      Planking secrets / Ron Shewchuk.

Includes index.
ISBN 1-55285-761-1

      1. Barbecue cookery. 2. Cookery (Smoked foods). 3. Outdoor cookery.
I. Title.
TX840.B3S553 2006   641.7'6   C2005-906776-4

The publisher acknowledges the financial support of the Government of Canada through the
Book Publishing Industry Development Program for our publishing activities.

CONTENTS

FOREWORD

Well, you didn't listen, did you? In Rockin' Ronnie's last book, *Barbecue Secrets*, I warned you to step back from the cookbook because the passionate relationship you'd inevitably be forging with your grill was going to get you in hot water—or, to be accurate, smouldering charcoal.

If instead of sensibly plunging ahead to the recipes, you read and remember cookbook forewords, you'll recall my prediction that you'd soon be in finger-lickin', lip-smackin' trouble. And now you're hooked. Was I right, or was I right? You spend your weekends fussing with coals and water-pans and looking out, beaming and misty-eyed, at the greasy grills and sooty smokers you consider almost as precious as your children.

Your spouse may or may not be relieved by this. But he or she is doubtless as addicted to eating your grilled or barbecued food as you are to making it. As for me, as wife of Ronnie, I'm soldiering on, now playing third fiddle not just to the outdoor cooking equipment cluttering the Shewchuk property but also to stacks of fragrant planks—cedar, alder, maple and oak.

Am I complaining? You bet—mainly because I can. But also because I'm certain that if, 20-odd years ago, I'd hooked up with somebody whose every recipe wasn't delicious, I'd be at least 50 pounds lighter.

Ah, well, that's a minor price to pay, considering the deliciousness I routinely enjoy. Cedar-planked salmon is one of the world's outstanding taste sensations, and living on the West Coast with a culinary artist-in-residence, it's available to me at the snap of a finger. Not to mention the planked pork loin, planked rack of lamb, planked peaches . . .

Wait a second—I sound like I'm gloating. Doubtless, you've now seen through my selfish scheme. I urged you to back away from *Barbecue Secrets*, but you didn't. The result? You've now got BBQ bragging rights. Now I'm telling you sternly that you'd best turn on your heel and walk away from *Planking Secrets*, maybe over to a book that will tell you how to poach cod in Evian water and garnish it with blanched clover. True, that dish will neither taste of anything nor fatten you up. But your dinner guests will soon drop away, and no one will ever see the new svelte you.

So what am I really saying here? Go for it! You may approach *Planking Secrets*. You may examine it. You may explore it. You may even cook from it. You may quickly master planking. And you may, many years hence, have this book pried from your cold, stiff hands on your way to an afterlife where cedar-planked salmon is always on the menu. In the meantime, what have I got against your being the architect of tremendously well-fed happiness, for yourself and others? Actually, nothing.

Bon appétit.

Kate Zimmerman

Kate Zimmerman
Barbecue and Planking Widow

P.S. Personal motto: When planning your own cremation, request the cedar chips. You'll feel like you're in a sauna. Maple, on the other hand, will only make you hungry.

INTRODUCTION

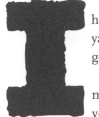I have seen the future of backyard cooking, and planking is going mainstream.

A highfalutin statement, I know. For many years plank-cooking has been an obscure technique practised by restaurateurs, anglers and nerdish foodies. But, thanks to the growing availability of quality cooking planks and exposure on network television, hundreds of thousands of people across North America have been discovering this easy, delicious grilling technique.

For a generation that has grown up on flavorless propane and gas grills, plank-cooking is a simple way to add the classic taste and aroma of wood smoke to meat. And, as you'll find out in this book, it also happens to be a great way to prepare vegetables, fresh fruit, nuts and even cheese.

The basic technique couldn't be simpler: soak a cedar or hardwood plank in water. Place it in a hot covered grill. When the plank starts to crackle and smoke, put whatever you want to cook on the plank and cover the grill. Soon you'll have juicy, perfectly cooked food infused with wonderful flavor.

I'll admit there's skepticism in some circles about planking. My friend and long-time mentor Bob Lyon is a correspondent for the *National Barbecue News* and a true barbecue purist. He says the popularity of cooking with planks—particularly in the U.S. Pacific Northwest, where cedar-planked salmon is a restaurant staple—is fueled by "misinformation for tourists and local gullibles." And another old pal, food writer and barbecue queen Kathy Richardier, says "it's a waste of perfectly good wood. The only

wood I advocate for food cooking is long sticks stuck with hot dogs or marshmallows over a campfire."

Unlike my curmudgeonly chums, some backyard cooks are attracted to the idea of plank-cooking but are reluctant to use planks on their grills, perhaps fearing the unknown or worrying about potential flare-ups and fires. The concept can be a bit daunting.

Well, I'm here to challenge the skeptics and calm the concerns of cautious grillers. With *Planking Secrets* I aim to tear down the Cedar Curtain and make plank-cooking safe, easy and fun for all backyard grillers. As you try out the techniques and recipes in this book, I'm convinced you'll quickly understand just how versatile planking can be, and how it can produce some of the most succulent dishes you've ever tasted. From classic planked salmon with whiskey-maple glaze to planked mushrooms with tarragon vinaigrette or planked pears in a pool of rhubarb compote, there's something in *Planking Secrets* for every taste and skill level.

So, read on. I predict that once you've had a good planking of your own, your backyard cooking will never be the same.

Yours forever in smoke,

Rockin' Ronnie a.k.a. Count Plankenstein

P.S. Find me at www.RonShewchuk.com.

A PLANK-COOKING PRIMER

Chapter 1

Cooking, or rather feeding people, is one of the most meaningful things a human being can do. And feeding people is about much more than opening a cookbook and following a recipe. It's about understanding the history, the culture and the science of food. In this chapter you'll learn the origins of plank-cooking and get a good idea of how this style of cooking works.

PLANKS FOR THE MEMORIES:
A Brief History of Plank-cooking

To chart the history of cooking with wood is to document the evolution of humankind. But the exact origins of plank-cooking are a little obscure.

We know, for example, that ancient aboriginal tribes on both sides of the North American continent would lash chunks of fish and meat to planks or stakes and lean them close to a fire. On the northwest coast, cooking salmon on planks by a roaring beach fire celebrated the bounty of the sea. Much of the catch would be smoked to preserve it for the winter, but freshly caught, freshly cooked salmon must have been as much of a delicacy back then as it is today —enhanced, of course, by fire and smoke.

On the east coast, the largest member of the herring family, the shad, makes its

annual spawning run up coastal rivers like the Hudson and the Nanticoke. The arrival of the shad marked the start of a rich fishery that, sadly, has been severely depleted, although shad are still harvested in limited numbers. In colonial times, the local natives taught European settlers how to cook shad fillets fastened to hardwood planks. The settlers adapted the technique, using nails to attach the fish to the planks, which are leaned against a rack running parallel to an open oak fire.

The tradition of the "shad planking," a celebratory feast, lives on and today marks the start of the political campaign season in New England. In the same spirit as the famed barbecue gatherings hosted by politicos and preachers in the American South, shad plankings have become a symbol of American democracy.

The technique of plank-cooking in restaurants and home kitchens gained popularity in the United States on both coasts in the mid-1800s. Early American cookbook authors Eliza Leslie and Fanny Farmer documented recipes for planked whitefish, shad and chicken. The technique was pretty simple: butter an oak plank (which would be reused), put the fish or meat on it and bake in a hot oven.

Meanwhile, hotel chefs in the Pacific Northwest began offering oven-planked dishes inspired by native cuisine, and to this day cedar-planked salmon is a popular dish in restaurants of the region.

This is where things get fuzzy. Despite an extensive search both on the Internet and in cooking reference books, I can't for the life of me find exactly how the plank made its way from the oven to the grill. It's an obvious and natural transition, but who did it first, and when?

The classic American covered charcoal grill wasn't invented until George Stephen welded together the first Weber Kettle in 1951. We also know that the first covered gas grill—which truly revolutionized backyard cooking—was introduced to the market by Modern Home Products in 1963. So plank-cooking on a covered grill began no more than 50 or 60 years ago. But was it someone on the east coast, adapting shad planking to a covered grill using

Shad fillets fastened to oak planks at a traditional New England shad planking
PHOTO COURTESY CHICONE RURITAN CLUB, VIENNA, MD

"Pacific Northwest natives later shared the plank-cooking method for wild salmon with European explorers and settlers. In the 1890s, the method gained popularity when some of the first hotels in the Northwest treated guests to this dramatic local cooking style."

From *Savory Flavors with Wood* by Nature's Cuisine

"In olden times shad was smoked on standing oak boards … This was called shad planking. The shad was cleaned and split open and nailed flat to the oak boards … The board was turned several times to get uniform cooking."

From the website of the Chicone Ruritan Club, an article on Nanticoke River shad planking

"Shad planking is a political event that takes place in Wakefield, Virginia, once every 4 years where would-be candidates, reporters, campaign workers, and locals gather to eat shad, drink beer, and kick off the state's electoral season with lighthearted speeches by politicians in attendance. The traditional event was originally a tribute to the start of the fishing season. However, it soon gained a political function, and in 1949 came under the control of the Wakefield Ruritan Club."

Wikipedia

"The only true planked salmon consists of fillets bound to a cedar plank, placed around an alder wood fire at a 15 degree angle away from the vertical and basted throughout the cooking process. The salmon fillets may be marinated or merely salted and peppered ahead of time."

Bob Lyon, Pacific Northwest columnist,

an oak board? Or was it someone in the west, planking the first salmon on a cedar shake? I have a standing offer to buy a case of delicious Okanagan wine for the person who can prove that they, or someone they know, was the first to plank-cook anything in a covered grill.

On a personal note, the first time I cooked on a plank was just a few years ago, after moving to British Columbia. Many Vancouver restaurants offer cedar-planked salmon on their menus, and I got a chance to taste it. At some point I came across the *Sticks & Stones* cookbook, by Canadian chef and grilling celebrity Ted Reader. Ted's planking techniques and innovative recipes got me hooked, and there was no turning back.

I remember the first time my wife, Kate, tasted cedar-planked salmon, fresh out of my propane grill. "My goodness, it's like having a sauna in my mouth!" she exclaimed. In that instant, she was hooked, too.

A JOURNEY TO THE ANCESTRAL HOME OF PLANK-COOKING

In the summer of 1986 Kate and I came to the west coast of British Columbia on a vacation with her parents, who were looking for a retirement home as far away from the dreaded winters of Ottawa as they could get. We all fell in love with a little town called Sechelt up the Sunshine Coast, a short ferry ride north of Vancouver. During that trip, my father-in-law, Bill, and I rented a 10-foot aluminum boat and went salmon fishing. With simple angling gear and a bucket of live herring for bait, we motored out to a group of small islands and put our hooks in the water.

Before long we had caught a couple of beautiful wild coho salmon, which put up an incredible fight as we reeled them in, flashing in the sun as they jumped out of the water. It

was the most exciting fishing experience I'd ever have. But even more memorable was the taste of that freshly caught salmon, which we ate within hours. Wrapped in foil and baked with just a little salt, pepper and lemon juice, it was succulent and delicious—like nothing we had tasted before.

We would all eventually move to the coast, the in-laws to Sechelt, and Kate and I to Vancouver. As a German sport fisherman once told me, explaining why he immigrated to British Columbia, "I came to catch the salmon, but the salmon caught me."

The salmon caught me, too. And not only the fish. I became interested in the role salmon has played in the rich history of the First Nations peoples. Before European settlers arrived, thousands of aboriginal people from many different tribes lived along the coast, harvesting the incredible bounty of seafood and plant life along the fjords and river inlets at the western edge of the coastal rainforest.

Ancient stories tell of rivers that were so thick with spawning salmon that a man could walk across on their backs.

With so much food, and such a moderate climate, there was time to build beautiful lodges, boats and totems and craft exquisite boxes, bowls and utensils —and develop extremely sophisticated fishing and cooking techniques.

The First Nations people made fishing hooks with bent wood and bone; fashioned fishing line from woven cedar bark; designed special rakes to sweep schools of herring into canoes; and built elaborate and ingenious traps at the mouths of streams to capture the salmon.

Salmon was, and still is today, at the heart of west coast aboriginal culture. Salmon sustained the native people through the winter, and the first salmon to return to the rivers to spawn marked the start of another prosperous year. Salmon were preserved and cooked in all kinds of ways, including wind-drying, smoking, boiling and pit-roasting. The first salmon of the season, filleted and fastened to a cedar post and roasted on an alder fire on the beach, was the direct ancestor of the salmon that you plank on your backyard grill today.

As I researched the history of plank-cooking for this book, I realized that to become a true planking expert I had to experience this ancient aboriginal barbecue technique first-hand. So I visited a place where the traditional practice is kept alive and well by the modern descendants of the Quw'utsun' people of Vancouver Island.

Historians estimate that the Quw'utsun' have been living in southern British Columbia and the Upper Puget Sound for more than 4,500 years. When the first European settlers arrived in the 1800s, there were close to 6,000 Quw'utsun' living in 13 villages. Today about 3,500 Quw'utsun' people live in the Cowichan Valley on Vancouver Island. Since 1990 they have showcased their culture to the world through the Quw'utsun' Cultural Centre, a campus-style facility near Duncan, British Columbia. The centre offers guests interpretive tours, exhibits of traditional artwork and the opportunity for non-aboriginals to sample traditional food. Their flagship culinary event is the salmon barbecue.

On a rainy day in the fall of 2005 I make a pilgrimage to the Cowichan Valley for a visit to the centre's Riverwalk Café, where executive chef Bev Antoine greets me. She's in the middle of preparations for a big salmon barbecue for an incoming group of Japanese tourists. Chef Antoine has been cooking at the centre since 1991 and has built a great team in her kitchen. Sous-chef Raymond

Chef Bev Antoine

Johnston is assigned to show me the salmon barbecue technique.

I arrive about two hours before the meal will be served, and Raymond is getting the salmon ready. He's got some beautiful fresh coho, about five or six pounds each. I watch him prepare one of the fish. He cuts the head off, then removes the backbone, keeping the whole fish intact in a kind of giant butterflied fillet. He carefully removes the remaining bones with a pair of needle-nose pliers.

Now it's time to light the fire. I join him in a trip out to the storage shed behind the restaurant, where we take turns splitting a bunch of alder and hauling it over to the nearby firepit. The wood is a little green, and we have to work hard to get it burning, but soon we have a nice crackling fire. Nature is cooperating and it has stopped raining.

Back to the kitchen, where Raymond mounts the fish fillets on piquin sticks—giant pairs of tongs made out of cedar posts that have been cut down the middle like old-fashioned wooden clothes pins. Raymond makes finger-sized incisions along the outside edge of each side of the salmon fillets and places the fillets between the tongs. To keep the fish straight and flat, he deftly inserts four cedar sticks through the incisions, across the width of the fillets. The last step is to close the tongs with some wire, firmly clamping the sticks against the salmon.

By the time Raymond is finished mounting all the coho on their sticks, the fire has died down to a perfect bed of hot alder coals. It smells incredible—the sweet smoke seems to transport us back thousands of years as we place the sticks in the sockets that line the pit. We tend the salmon, turning it every 15 minutes or so as our lunch guests begin to gather around the fire, taking pictures and chatting. Within an hour the red flesh of the coho has turned orangey pink and is glistening with hot juices.

It's time for the lunch service. Raymond and I take the piquin sticks out of their sockets and carry the salmon back to the kitchen. He cuts the fillets in half and places them on long cedar planks along with bowls of roasted potatoes, steamed vegetables and a salad of local greens drizzled with blackberry vinaigrette. I join in with the kitchen staff as we work in pairs to carry the planks into the dining hall and dramatically present them to the assembled lunch guests. The Japanese, who aren't used to seeing salmon like this, are in awe.

Back in the kitchen, I grab a fork and pull a chunk of belly meat off one of the fillets. The flavor of the salmon has been touched lightly by the alder smoke. The flesh is juicy and perfectly succulent, with lots of flavor even though the fish has not even been salted. I close my eyes as I chew, thinking about

how it must have felt to eat salmon like this after a long winter of surviving on preserved food.

That feast would have been much more than a meal—it was a celebration of the renewal of nature and recognition of the recurring gift of the salmon to the coastal people. In a book called *Indian Fishing: Early Methods on the Northwest Coast*, author Hilary Stewart quotes a prayer that would have been recited at the first sight of the salmon:

> *Welcome, friend Swimmer,*
> *we have met again in good health.*
> *Welcome, Supernatural One,*
> *you, Long-Life-Maker,*
> *For you come to set me right again*
> *as is always done by you.*

When you cook using the recipes from this book, and taste the food that has been enhanced with the smoke of the plank, think about your family, your friends, your health, your work, and the nourishing, delicious meal you're enjoying and take a moment to be thankful for it all.

Raymond Johnson puts another log on the fire.

THE BASICS: Plank-cooking Made Easy

Why plank in the first place? If you want smoky flavor you can use a charcoal grill, or toss some soaked wood chips into your gas grill. If you want to slow-roast something you can put it in a smoker, or use indirect heat on your grill by turning off the burner under your roast or moving the briquettes to either side.

Well, it turns out there are distinct advantages to grilling with planks.

- **Planking adds great flavor without the mess.** Ever try to clean a grill that's got salmon skin stuck all over it? With planking, food never touches the cooking grate. If you're adding flavor with wood chips, you're going to get ashes, which have to be cleaned up eventually. Planks stay intact throughout the cooking process. When you're finished, you take the plank off and you're done.

- **The plank helps cook food gently.** A soaked plank is going to throw off smoke, but it also produces steam, which moderates the heat and helps the food retain its moisture. The plank also insulates whatever you're cooking from the direct heat of the grill, cooking food more gently and evenly.

- **Plank-cooking is spectacular.** There's a theatrical aspect to planking that plays into the need for backyard cooks (especially men) to show off to their spouses and guests. You've got smoke. You've got campfire-like crackling. Sometimes you've got fire around the edges of the plank, which has to be expertly sprayed to put it out. And, with planked salmon in particular, you've got a magnificent way of presenting and serving the fish, right on the beautifully charred plank.

- **Planking is low-fat.** I'm actually not so sure that's an advantage, but for some people I suppose it's nice to know that you don't need to add oil or fat to the food to enhance the flavor or prevent sticking.

PLANKING ➤ SECRET ≈

To reuse, or not to reuse? That is a good question, and the easy answer is the one my mentor Ted Reader gives: "Planks have two uses, one on your grill, the other in your fireplace." The more complicated answer is that planks can be used multiple times as long as you wash them thoroughly between uses and then store them in a place with good air circulation so they won't get moldy. Hardwood planks like oak or maple stand up best to multiple uses because they're very dense. Cedar, because it's lighter and more porous, tends to get quite charred and crumbly on the first use and therefore doesn't recycle well.

PLANKING GEAR

Like all great pastimes, plank-cooking requires a certain amount of gear, most of which is already in your grilling arsenal. Here are the essentials.

Planks: There are all kinds and sizes of grilling planks on the market today and you can get them at gourmet food and kitchen stores, supermarkets and home improvement centers. The best kind of wood for beginners is cedar because it soaks up more water than other woods, which makes flare-ups less likely. The ideal size of a grilling plank is about 7 inches wide by 12 inches long (18 by 30 cm), and between 1/4 and 5/8 inch thick (0.6 to 1.5 cm). You want a plank that's not too long to fit in your covered grill and big enough to hold what you want to cook, with a little space on all sides (this protects the food from charring in case you get flare-ups along the edges). Old-timers, purists and cheapskates will tell you the best way to get planks is to go to your local lumberyard or home improvement center and buy cedar shakes or fencing planks (make sure they're untreated, of course), which you can then saw to whatever length you want. Whatever you do, don't use softwoods like pine, spruce or fir for planking. They're too resiny and their smoke imparts a bad taste.

Covered charcoal or gas grill: Just about any kind of covered grill will do, and even the small portables work fine. As with other styles of grilling and barbecue, you're going to get more flavor using a charcoal-fired cooker. But most households in North America have propane or natural gas grills, and they work just fine with a plank.

Space: Grilling with planks produces quite a bit of smoke, which is going to cause you trouble if your grill is in a tight, semi-enclosed space like a covered deck or an apartment balcony. You also need to be far enough away from your neighbors, or at least downwind from them, so you don't smoke them out of their houses.

Fire extinguisher: Every cook should have one in the kitchen, and 2 if the kitchen is far away from where you keep your grill. You may never have to use it, but you'll regret it if you have to put out a fire without one.

Spray bottle filled with water: I'm talking about your basic garden-variety spray bottle, the kind people use for spraying house-plants or moistening clothes before ironing. You need this to put out the little flare-ups that are inevitable with this style of cooking, especially if you didn't soak your plank for very long before putting it on the grill.

Sturdy tongs: The longer, the better. You'll use these for placing food on the plank, but you can also remove the plank with the food on it by grabbing it with a good set of tongs (this only works for lighter fare, and on planks that aren't too burnt).

1 or 2 wide, long metal spatulas: The easiest, safest way to take a plank off the grill is with 2 spatulas. This gives you the most control and allows you to pick up planks that have been weakened by charring.

Large baking pans or cookie sheets: You can transfer a hot, smoldering plank to a baking pan or cookie sheet to let it cool down before serving.

Large stainless steel serving dish: Sometimes the most attractive and simplest way to serve planked food is to present it and carve it right on the plank. But you need to put the plank on something that won't melt or burn.

Meat thermometers: I recommend you have two kinds: an instant-read thermometer and a probe-style digital thermometer. You can poke the instant-read device into whatever you're cooking to find out the internal temperature within a few seconds. For larger cuts, a probe-style thermometer will give you an ongoing, live reading of the core temperature of your meat without having to open the cover of your grill. Some of the higher-end models come with radio transmitters and remote devices that allow you to monitor the internal temperature of your meat from as far as 50 feet (15 m) away. The good ones have alarm settings so your remote will beep when your meat is ready to take off the grill. Maverick brand remote thermometers are the best I've tried. They're easy to use and reliable, unlike many others on the market today.

Chamber thermometer: Most grills nowadays have a chamber thermometer that gives you a pretty good idea of the temperature inside the cooker. If yours doesn't have one, a standard oven thermometer can be used. Just sit it on the plank right next to the food for an accurate reading.

Silicone basting brush: If you don't have a silicone basting brush, I recommend that you add one to your gear collection immediately. This is a huge upgrade from your basic pig-bristle paintbrush-style basters. They hold more sauce, spread it more evenly, stand up to very high temperatures and clean up in the dishwasher.

Drip pans: When you're planking (or grilling) large, fatty cuts of meat it pays to put a drip pan beneath the cooking grate to avoid flare-ups and keep your grill clean. I find the large-size rectangular disposable aluminum trays work best.

Is Untreated ↪ Really ↩ Untreated?

When I've gone to a lumberyard to buy untreated planks to use for cooking, I've always assumed they don't have any unwanted chemicals on them. Even so, I've made sure to rinse the planks thoroughly before using them. But I have since talked with experts in the field, and they tell me a couple of things that might give pause to those who want to cut their own planks. First, there are some lumber mills that, as a matter of course, spray all the wood coming out of the mill with an agent that helps resist mold and mildew. Who knows whether that's good for your health? On top of that, when you buy an untreated plank, do you know how and where it's been stored? If it has been on a rack, exposed to the rain, with poisonous treated wood above it, have the chemicals leached out of the preserved wood to contaminate the untreated planks below? If this worries you, always look for planks meant for cooking that say they are untreated and have "food-grade" on the label.

COMMON TYPES OF PLANKS

WOOD	FLAVORS	USES
Cedar (If you're buying it at a lumberyard, you must specify untreated western red cedar.)	Spicy, exotic, mildly astringent. Like having a sauna in your mouth.	Goes best with sweeter meats like salmon, pork and lamb, and tree fruits like peaches and pears, but try it with other foods, including veggies, nuts and cheese.
Apple, apricot, peach and other fruitwoods	Mild, sweet, fruity.	Great for pork, poultry, game and seafood.
Alder	A west coast classic. Mild, delicate, dry, with hints of vanilla; a bit like oak but much lighter.	Perfect with salmon and other seafood but also good with almost anything else.
Cherry	More flavorful than other fruitwoods, cherry imparts a distinct, sweet, smoky taste.	Ideal for poultry, lamb and game.
Hickory	The most recognizable flavor in all of barbecue, hickory is the most versatile cooking wood.	Excellent with pork, salmon, red meat, cheese and nuts. The intense flavor conjures up traditional southern-style cooking. Anything cooked with hickory becomes a comfort food. Not as good for more delicate meats, fish or vegetables.
Maple	We all know the smooth, sweet smell of maple because a lot of bacon is flavored with maple smoke.	A classic flavor that works with almost anything you want to cook, but is best suited to pork and poultry.
Oak	The taste of Texas barbecue (especially red oak). Oak adds a strong, dry, slightly astringent flavor.	Best with beef, but works with almost anything.
Mesquite	The strongest flavor of all the hardwoods, it's the classic taste of the American Southwest.	Perfect with pork and beef, it might be too strong for milder and more delicate foods.
Other woods	You can use any hardwood to plank-cook food, but the more exotic you get, the more expensive the wood can be (try buying a walnut plank and you'll see what I mean). Apparently Hawaiian guava wood is superb (but expensive).	

TEN STEPS TO PLANKING PERFECTION

Planking is as easy as one, two, three: soak the plank, preheat it on the grill, put your food on. There's just a little more to it than that. Follow these 10 simple steps to perfect planking every time.

Step 1

Soak the plank. This step is a must unless you want to convert your grill into an inferno. Ideally, soak your plank overnight, but I recommend you soak planks for at least 1 hour before use. (In a pinch you can get away with an hour of soaking time, but you've got to be extra vigilant to catch and put out flare-ups during cooking.)

NOTE: Longer soaking is especially important with hardwoods like alder, maple and oak, which are much denser than cedar. Planks float, so to soak them you need to weigh them down. I use a rock from my garden, but you can use a container of water, a heavy jar or jug, or a brick. Don't use cans, because they rust.

Step 2

Get your food ready to go. Have all your prep work done before you start the grill. You don't want a plank that's ready for the food but food that's not ready for the plank. By the time you've caught up, the plank will literally have gone up in smoke.

Step 3

Preheat your grill. Prepare the grill for medium-high direct cooking. For a gas grill, this means all burners are on, at about three-quarters full, for about 5 minutes. For a charcoal grill, you want a fairly full, fresh, hot layer of charcoal—maybe 30 briquettes. This will take 15 to 20 minutes.

Step 4

Take the plank out of the soaking water, rinse it well under a tap and place it on the cooking grate. Once you've got the plank on the grill, close the cover immediately. If the plank has a smooth and a rough side, put the rough side facing down.

Step 5

Let the plank heat up inside the grill. In about 4 or 5 minutes you'll hear the plank start to gently pop and

The longer you soak a plank, the more likely it is to warp when you preheat it on the grill. For many applications this doesn't matter much, and sometimes a slight curve to the plank enhances the final presentation. But in other cases, you want a flat plank so things like mushrooms, baked apples or tomatoes won't roll off. Two tricks here: first, avoid excessive warping by soaking your plank for an hour or even less if you're careful to manage flare-ups with a spray bottle. Second, place a clean brick on your plank when you first put it on the grill and the plank will stay flat while it's preheating.

When you take a plank off the grill, after you've removed the cooked food, always douse it with water or spray it with a hose until it stops smoking (unless you're going to serve the food on the plank, in which case you should wait till it stops smoking before bringing it into the house). Never lay a smouldering plank down on something flammable or meltable, like a plastic tablecloth.

If you need to use 2 or even 3 planks at a time, make sure that you leave at least an inch (2.5 cm) of open space between them to allow for good smoke circulation.

Sprinkle a layer of kosher salt on the plank just before you put your food on. This helps prevent whatever you're cooking from sticking to the plank. Some planking experts also recommend painting the plank with cooking oil just before putting food on.

You can add other liquids to your soaking water for more flavor. Try apple juice, wine, Jack Daniel's, rum or flavored vinegars.

Plastic storage tubs work best for soaking planks, but large lasagna pans will also do.

Store your planks in a cool, dry, well-ventilated area to prevent mold and mildew. Planks from freshly cut, live trees should be stacked with slats between them and seasoned for a year.

If you want to reuse a plank, wash it with mild soap and warm water immediately after use. When the plank is dry, sand the surface to open the grain and release more flavor the next time you cook with it.

crackle, and you'll see some smoke coming out of the grill. Don't wait too long or your plank will go up in flames, especially on a gas grill.

Step 6

Put your food on the plank. Leave at least a 1- or 2-inch (2.5- to 5-cm) margin of wood around the edge.

Step 7

Immediately turn the heat down. This applies mainly to gas grills. You should turn it down to medium or medium-low as soon as the plank is ready. This allows the food to cook more gently and reduces flare-ups. You're looking for an internal chamber temperature of 350–500°F (175–260°C). I know that's a big range, but some gas grills just don't get much below 500°F (260°C). For most applications, the more moderate the heat, the better the result.

Step 8

Closely monitor the grill. Take care to spray water on flare-ups if they occur. (Don't open the lid too often as that will increase the oxygen and encourage the plank to burn.)

Step 9

Take the planked food, and the plank, off the grill. You can do this 2 ways: take the food off the plank and then take the plank off the grill, or take the plank off with the food on it (a great way to present salmon).

Step 10

Put out the plank. Make sure the plank you're using is safely out of the grill. Dunk it in water or spray it with a hose to make sure it's completely out.

CAUTION

Keep an eye on food while it's being planked. Never stray too far from your grill while you're plank-cooking. If it's billowing giant clouds of smoke, your plank is on fire and you need to be there with your spray bottle. (This circumstance is rare, and it's usually caused by an undersoaked plank in a too-hot grill with very fatty meat on the wood.) If you get distracted and your plank is completely in flames, a spray bottle might not do. You might need to pour a cup of water along the burning edges of the plank to subdue the fire.

HOW TO TELL WHEN YOUR MEAT IS DONE

Is it done yet? This question haunts anyone who has ruined an expensive piece of meat by overcooking. Every grill, and every plank and every piece of meat is different —and so is every day when it comes to weather conditions. With so many variables, adhering strictly to the time specified in a recipe isn't the best approach. Use the times in this book as guidelines only, and test your meat for doneness using either the feel of the meat, or the internal temperature as measured by an instant-read or probe thermometer.

Here's how to test by feel: prod the meat with your finger to check the springiness of the flesh. If it gives easily to the touch, it's quite underdone. If it springs back from your touch, it's time to take it off the heat. (With practice you'll learn how to equate the degree of springiness with the doneness of the meat.) And if the meat is hard to the touch, it's turned into pet food. Don't let this happen to you!

MEAT	INTERNAL TEMPERATURE
Poultry	160°F (71°C) (or until juices run clear when you pierce the meat)
Beef or Lamb	125°F (52°C) for rare 140°F (60°C) for medium rare 160°F (71°C) for overdone
Pork	140°F (60°C) for perfectly done 160°F (71°C) for dry and crumbly
Salmon or other fish	135°F (57°C) for perfectly done 160°F (71°C) for flaky and dry

ANOTHER CAUTION

Always turn off the grill after you've taken the food off the plank. I learned this lesson the hard way. One time I was planking some salmon and had 2 planks in the grill. I took the salmon off, but absent-mindedly left the grill on, with the planks still inside. The heat from the grill, combined with a strong, dry crosswind, turned the grill into a furnace and melted the cooking grates. Molten metal actually dripped out of the grill onto the stand below. Since then I always turn the heat off and take the planks off the grill!

For extra flavor, place a bed of fresh herbs on the plank just before you put the food on.

For extra-large pieces of meat or large volumes of food, you can use multiple planks, or wooden slats instead of planks. If using slats, just lay them across the grill, leaving a space between each for circulation. Don't forget to soak them well beforehand.

Get to know your grill. Every grill has hot spots and cooler areas. Know where they are and use them to your advantage. For example, if you're planking or grilling cuts of meat that are different sizes, put the larger ones on the hotter part of the grill so they all cook at the same rate. Or, if you know someone likes their meat extra-rare, place it on the cooler part of the grill.

Hardwood planks, because they have a tighter grain, are easier to reuse. Wash the plank with warm soapy water as soon as it has cooled, rinse well and be sure there is good air circulation while the plank is drying.

THE SCIENCE OF PLANKING

When wood burns or smolders, it releases smoke into the air. Smoke is made up of three things: little soot particles (which make smoke look gray or black), steam and aromatic hydrocarbons—the magical, invisible vapors that contain the essence of the wood flavor. When smoke surrounds a piece of food inside a covered grill, the aromatic vapors penetrate it and impart the distinctive smoky flavors that we love.

Because gas grills don't produce any smoke, they also don't add any flavor. That's why planking is becoming so popular.

When you cook on a plank in your grill, the flame of the burners heats the bottom of the plank. Even if you don't see much smoke coming out of your grill, the invisible vapors are still coming out of the plank and flavoring the food.

You'll know the vapors have been doing their work when you see a smoke ring around a piece of meat. This red layer results when natural nitrates react with the hemoglobin in the muscles, fixing the red color.

Another bit of science is what happens to meat when it's heated. There are long strands of protein in the muscle fibers. When they are exposed to heat, they coil up, which is why the meat firms up as it cooks. If you cook a piece of meat too fast at too high a temperature, the proteins coil up too tightly and squeeze the precious juices out of the muscle fibers. That's one reason that you want to let meat rest. The proteins uncoil, the fibers relax, the meat retains its juices and the texture is nice and succulent. With intense heat, the protein strands can actually break, which makes the texture crumbly. Anyone who has bitten into an overcooked, mealy chicken breast has experienced this principle in action. Yuk!

Now you know why plank-cooking works so well. The plank protects and insulates the meat, preventing it from cooking too fast, and the result is a moister, more tender product.

PLANKING LIMITATIONS

Like every cooking style, planking has its limitations, although the more I grill using planks, the more I find it to be an incredibly versatile technique. But here are the drawbacks.

- **Little or no charring or searing.** There are no grill marks with plank-cooking, although it's easy to sear a steak or chicken breast on the cooking grate just before you place it on the plank.

- **Limited area to cook on.** If you want to cook for a crowd, you may need to use 2 or even 3 planks at a time, and especially with bought planks, that's a little pricy.

- **Hard to cook on short notice.** Plank-cooking goes against the convenience of grilling. You've got to soak the plank for at least 1 hour, so it's not for backyard cooks in a big hurry.

- **All that smoke.** You might love to plank every day, but your neighbors might not appreciate it.

RONNIE'S PANTRY
Essential Ingredients and Recipes

Chapter 2

ost of this chapter is drawn from my first book, *Barbecue Secrets*. These essential ingredients and classic recipes have stood the test of time and apply just as well to plank-cooking as to traditional barbecue or conventional grilling. The pantry items are the foundation of my style of cooking, and the recipes are a tasty, versatile collection of marinades, rubs and sauces that you can adapt to your individual taste.

WHAT TO KEEP IN YOUR CUPBOARD

Asian sauces: Light and dark soy, toasted sesame oil, oyster sauce, black bean sauce and chili garlic sauce should be in your pantry. Use them in marinades, combine them to make an Asian finishing glaze, mix them with mayo for a flavorful dip, or just paint them on meat as you grill it. A note about soy sauce: I prefer the naturally brewed Japanese soy sauce (Kikkoman is a good brand) because it has a richer, milder flavor.

Black peppercorns: If you haven't already done so, throw out any prepackaged ground pepper in your pantry. Pepper loses its aromatic oils shortly after being ground, so always use whole peppercorns and grind them in a pepper mill or, if you need a large amount, use a spice mill or coffee grinder. Use finely ground pepper in rubs and a coarser grind for coating steaks and roasts.

Chiles, ground: These are one of the essential flavor components of great barbecue. Use them in everything: sauces, marinades, rubs, dips and dressings. Cut half-and-half with kosher salt and sprinkle on hot buttered corn on the cob. Add to guacamole and salsa for extra flavor and heat. Be sure to use the real stuff—don't waste your money on store-bought blended chili powder!

Cooking spray: For spraying grills and food about to go on the grill.

Chipotles in adobo sauce: This is common in Latin American pantries and widely available in the Mexican food section of most supermarkets. Dried chipotles are reconstituted and stewed in a tomato-based sauce and packaged in little tins. One or 2 chipotles add a wonderful, hot, smoky flavor to sauces and marinades.

Cumin seeds: Cumin seeds are available just about everywhere these days, and you can buy big bags of them in the Indian spices section of your supermarket. This is one of my favorite spices, with a dark, earthy, slightly smoky taste and pungent aroma. Use them whole to add an interesting texture to dishes and give a little burst of flavor when you bite into them. For most uses I recommend toasting cumin seeds (dry-frying them for a few minutes in a hot sauté pan) before adding them to whatever you're cooking. There's nothing like the taste of freshly toasted cumin seeds ground in a spice mill or coffee grinder!

Extra virgin olive oil: There isn't much room for olive oil in traditional barbecue, but for grilled and planked foods there's nothing like a last-minute drizzle of fruity extra virgin olive oil and a squeeze of lemon to brighten flavors and enhance the richness of your cooking.

Flavored oils: French toasted walnut oil, truffle oil, lime-infused olive oil and chili-flavored oil add so much to salads and marinades, making it easy to add a distinctive and unusual flavor to everyday fare. A couple of tablespoons of flavored oil, a squeeze of fresh lemon or lime juice, a little dollop of Dijon, some finely minced shallots and a pinch of salt and pepper makes a quick dressing that will amaze your guests.

Granulated garlic and onion: Lots of cooks frown on powdered seasonings, and I don't blame them. They can often taste rancid and bitter, especially when they're not fresh. But granulated garlic and onion are different. They have a wonderful texture and a rich, roasted taste that adds an intense flavor to grilled and barbecued food. I find myself adding a bit of granulated onion to almost everything I cook nowadays for an extra dimension of flavor. (Since my first book, *Barbecue Secrets*, was published I've had many people ask me where to get granulated garlic and onion. I get mine at ethnic markets, and you can usually find it in the Indian section of bigger supermarkets. But I've found in recent years that what's sold as garlic and onion powder in most supermarkets is really the granulated product. Just look for a sand-like, rather than powdery, consistency and you won't go wrong.)

Herbs, dried: The modern kitchen tends to shy away from dried herbs in favor of their aromatic and delicate fresh counterparts, but good dried herbs (that is, ones that haven't spent the last 7 years in the back of your spice cupboard) add a richness and complexity to food that fresh herbs can't. I often like to combine fresh herbs with their dried counterparts to create a big, balanced flavor with an earthy, bitter bottom and a crisp aromatic brightness.

Ketchup: This gives Kansas City-style barbecue sauces their classic sweetness and glossy, thick texture.

Kosher salt: Please, please, please throw out all your cheap iodized salt, which is too powdery and has a chemical aftertaste from the iodine that is added to prevent goiter. Trust me. You're not going to get goiter, a disease caused by iodine deficiency. I'm sure we all get enough iodine from the salt in the processed food we eat! You can get kosher salt at almost any specialty food shop and in many supermarkets these days. Be sure you get a brand like Diamond Crystal, which has a perfect graininess. Avoid kosher salts that are very coarse; these are mainly used for pickling. Kosher salt also has a less salty, more well-rounded flavor. If you want to get even fancier, use lovely white crystalline Malden salt from England, or grayish-brown, minerally *fleur de sel* from France, for putting that finishing sprinkle on food just before you serve it.

Lemons and limes: Don't bother with bottled lime or lemon juice. The real thing is so much better! Always keep a few of each of these on hand to add tang to a sauce or salad, to squeeze over meat or vegetables fresh off the grill, or to chew on between shots of tequila!

Mustard: Good old ballpark-style prepared mustard is an essential component of barbecued meat, but you should also have some Dijon in your fridge. Flavored mustards like wasabi-lime or honey mustard add a nice twist to marinades, mayo and dressings. Grainy mustard gives sauces and glazes an extra bit of texture.

Nuts: I like to keep bags of pecan halves, pine nuts, pumpkin seeds and slivered almonds in the freezer. Quickly toast them in a frying pan or put them on a cookie sheet for a few minutes under your broiler or in a 350°F (175°C) oven and sprinkle them on a salad or piece of grilled fish to add some crunch and flavor.

Seasoned salts: Garlic salt, onion salt, celery salt and steak-house seasoning salt are important components of barbecue rubs.

Sours: White vinegar, cider vinegar, red and white wine vinegars and balsamic vinegar are good to have around. It's all about the balance of salt, sour, bitter, sweet and savory.

Sweets: Honey, maple syrup, granulated sugar, brown sugar and molasses add an important dimension to sauces, marinades and dressings.

PLANKING ⤳ SECRET ⤳

Don't plank everything. Part of the joy of planking is the novelty. As my son said, upon being presented with a particularly smoky planked peach, "Dad, you know, everything doesn't have to taste like barbecue. There are other styles of cooking. Sometimes it's nice just to taste a plain peach." 'Nuff said.

championship RUB
BARBECUE (a.k.a. Bob's rub)

Makes about 3 cups | 750 mL

This is the rub my team, Rockin' Ronnie's Butt Shredders, uses in competition. Bob Lyon, the granddaddy of barbecue in the Pacific Northwest, shared this at a barbecue workshop that first introduced us to the joys of real barbecue and inspired us to become barbecue champions. It follows a rule of thumb that's worth remembering: a third, a third, a third. Which means one-third sugar, one-third seasoned salts, and one-third dried herbs and spices.

1 cup | 250 mL white sugar

1/4 cup | 50 mL celery salt

1/4 cup | 50 mL garlic salt

1/4 cup | 50 mL onion salt

1/4 cup | 50 mL seasoning salt (I like Lawrey's)

1/3 cup | 75 mL chili powder (use a commercial blend, or if you want an edge, try a combination of real ground chiles like ancho, poblano, New Mexico or guajillo)

1/3 cup | 75 mL black pepper

1/3 cup | 75 mL paprika

To this basic rub add as much heat as you want using cayenne pepper, hot paprika or ground chipotles. Then add 2 or 3 signature spices to suit whatever you're cooking or your personal taste, like powdered thyme, oregano, cumin, sage, powdered ginger, etc. Add only 1 to 3 tsp (5 to 15 mL) of each signature seasoning so as not to overpower the rub. Mix well, seal in an airtight container and store in a cool, dry place.

PLANKING ☞ SECRET ☜

Although many people use the terms "barbecue" and "grilling" interchangeably, for some folks, particularly in the American south and on the competitive barbecue circuit, there's a big difference. To "grill" is to cook food on a hot cooking grate for a short time, directly over a gas or charcoal fire. The noun "barbecue" means meat, often pork, that's cooked over a low, smoldering hardwood or charcoal fire for a long time, tenderizing the meat and infusing it with smoky flavor. Plank-cooking is a hybrid: the cooking temperature is fairly high, but the food is shielded from direct heat and the smoldering plank gives it a barbecue flavor.

TEXAS style RUB

Makes about 2 cups | 500 mL

Everyone has a friend of a friend of a friend who knows someone in Texas with a great rub recipe. This one came to me through fellow Butt Shredder Ian "Big Daddy" Baird. The cayenne pepper gives it a nice burn. Use it as an all-purpose rub. It's especially good with beef.

3/4 cup | 175 mL paprika

1/4 cup | 50 mL kosher salt

1/4 cup | 50 mL sugar

1/4 cup | 50 mL ground black pepper

1/4 cup | 50 mL chili powder

2 Tbsp | 25 mL garlic powder

2 Tbsp | 25 mL onion powder

1 Tbsp | 15 mL cayenne pepper, or to taste

Mix well, seal in an airtight container and store in a cool, dry place.

ROCKIN' RONNIE'S GRILLINGrub

Makes about 1 cup | 250 mL

I like to use this combination of seasonings for everyday grilling. It perfectly balances the earthiness of the toasted cumin, the sharpness of ground pepper, the smokiness and heat of the ground chipotles and the natural sweetness of the ancho chile, granulated onion and garlic.

4 Tbsp | 50 mL kosher salt

1 tsp | 5 mL ground black pepper

2 Tbsp | 25 mL ground toasted cumin seeds

1 Tbsp | 15 mL ground oregano

2 Tbsp | 25 mL granulated onion

1 Tbsp | 15 mL granulated garlic

2 Tbsp | 25 mL ancho chile powder

1 tsp | 5 mL ground chipotles (if you can't find this, substitute cayenne pepper)

1 tsp | 5 mL dried parsley

Mix well, seal in an airtight container and store in a cool, dry place.

mediterranean dried HERB RUB

These days food lovers shy away from dried herbs in favor of the fresh ones that are so readily available. We tend to associate unpleasantly stale, dirty flavors with dried herbs, but that's probably because we use them so rarely that the ones in our pantry are too old. Dried herbs, when used within a few months of being purchased, can add a wonderful earthiness and complexity to grilled foods. In fact, the high heat of grilling often destroys the delicate flavors of fresh herbs. In most cases fresh herbs, other than the very strong rosemary and sage, are best used after your meat is off the grill, as a finely chopped sprinkle to add color and aroma.

1 Tbsp | 15 mL dried (not powdered) oregano

1 Tbsp | 15 mL dried mint

1 Tbsp | 15 mL dried basil

1 Tbsp | 15 mL dried rosemary

1 tsp | 5 mL dried parsley

Mix all ingredients well.

To use with meat, first season whatever you're cooking with salt and pepper, then coat lightly with Dijon mustard (or alternatively, marinate the meat in olive oil, lemon juice, Dijon and maybe some chopped fresh rosemary). Once your meat is either coated with mustard or out of the marinade, give it a light dusting of granulated garlic, and then sprinkle the dry herb rub all over the meat, pressing it in with your hands to help it stick. Let it sit for 10 or 15 minutes to moisten the herbs a bit before putting the meat on the grill.

To use with vegetables, toss whatever veggies you want to roast with some kosher salt and olive oil. Then add some of the herb rub and toss about until everything is nicely coated. After they're grilled, finish with a squeeze of fresh lemon.

HERBED wet RUB

Makes about 2 cups | 500 mL

This is a cross between a marinade and a paste. It's superb on any meat and meaty fish like salmon or swordfish. Thin it a bit with more olive oil and you can toss vegetables in it to roast on the grill. It's even great tossed with some fresh cooked pasta.

**2 cups | 500 mL loosely packed fresh chopped herbs
(use equal parts of fresh Italian parsley, mint, basil,
cilantro, baby dill, sage, or any combination that goes
with what you want to grill)**

6 cloves garlic, peeled

1 shallot, coarsely chopped

1 Tbsp | 15 mL chopped chives

1 tsp | 5 mL Dijon mustard

1 tsp | 5 mL kosher salt

**up to 1 cup | 250 mL oil (extra virgin if you're going
with a Mediterranean theme, or a more neutral-flavored
oil if you're cooking Asian or Southwestern)**

Combine the herbs, garlic, shallot, chives, mustard and salt in a food processor and whiz until everything is finely chopped. Keep the processor running and slowly add the oil until the mixture looks like a thin paste (or a very thick marinade.) Coat whatever you're grilling with the mixture and let sit for 1/2 to 1 hour for veggies and seafood and anywhere from 2 hours to overnight for meat. This rub doesn't keep well, so make it right when you need it.

mediterranean MARINADE

Makes enough for a couple of racks of lamb, four chicken breasts or eight chicken thighs

Don't let the anchovy scare you. It adds a wonderful depth of flavor, and the end product doesn't taste fishy at all.

1/2 cup | 125 mL extra virgin olive oil

1 Tbsp | 15 mL Dijon mustard

1 Tbsp | 15 mL olive paste or 6 calamata olives, pitted and chopped

1 anchovy fillet

1 Tbsp | 15 mL coarsely chopped fresh rosemary

1 Tbsp | 15 mL chopped fresh basil

1 Tbsp | 15 mL chopped fresh mint

1 Tbsp | 15 mL Mediterranean Dried Herb Rub (see page 32)

juice of 1 lemon

1 Tbsp | 15 mL balsamic vinegar

Combine all ingredients in a food processor and whiz until blended but not totally puréed.

complicated BUT DELICIOUS TERIYAKI sauce

Makes about 8 cups | 2 L

This homemade teriyaki sauce, which I have slightly adapted from a recipe by famed Vancouver chef Trevor Hooper, has dimensions of flavor that make the extra work more than worthwhile. It stores for several months in the fridge. It's great as a marinade for meat or seafood, as a sauce for stir-fries, or just drizzled on steamed rice.

$1\frac{1}{2}$ **cups | 375 mL sake**

$1\frac{1}{2}$ **cups | 375 mL mirin**

2 cups | 500 mL brown sugar

4 cups | 1 L soy sauce

1/2 cup | 125 mL tamari sauce

1 small onion, chopped

1 shallot, chopped

4 cloves garlic, chopped

one 2-inch | 5-cm piece fresh ginger, chopped

1 orange, skin on, chopped

1 small pear, chopped

1 small leek, split, washed thoroughly and chopped

Combine ingredients in a medium saucepan and bring to a low boil. Cook until the mixture is reduced by about 20 percent. Cool, strain into a large jar or bottle and refrigerate.

ASIAN poultry BRINE

Makes enough for 2 cut-up chickens or a dozen thighs

My barbecue team has used this very successfully in competition. The high salt content makes it more of a brine than a marinade. It gives the poultry a nice saltiness and a rich Asian flavor. I marinate duck overnight in this; for milder-tasting chicken, a couple of hours is all you need. Pat excess moisture from the meat after you've taken it out of the marinade and then use a barbecue rub doctored with Asian flavors, like powdered ginger and five-spice powder.

1½ cups | 375 mL water

1 cup | 250 mL soy sauce

1/2 cup | 125 mL sherry or vermouth

1/2 cup | 125 mL apple or pineapple juice

1/4 cup | 50 mL brown sugar

1/4 cup | 50 mL coarse salt

2 cloves garlic, pressed or crushed

1 shallot, minced

1 medium onion, thinly sliced

2 Tbsp | 25 mL grated fresh ginger

1 tsp | 5 mL sesame oil

pinch ground cloves

pinch five-spice powder

Combine all ingredients, stirring well to dissolve the salt and sugar.

marinade FOR PORK

Makes enough marinade for up to 2 lb | 1 kg of pork chops or whole tenderloins

Pork tastes great no matter how you prepare it, but this sweet, aromatic marinade nicely offsets its richness and gives it an exotic edge.

1/4 cup | 50 mL soy sauce

2 Tbsp | 25 mL dry sherry

2 Tbsp | 25 mL honey

2 Tbsp | 25 mL brown sugar

1 tsp | 5 mL salt

1/2 tsp | 2 mL crushed anise seed

1/2 tsp | 2 mL ground cinnamon

1/8 tsp | 0.5 mL ground cloves

1 Tbsp | 15 mL grated fresh ginger

Combine ingredients in a saucepan and heat gently until the sugar has dissolved, then cool. Marinate the meat for at least 1 hour, or overnight in the fridge if you want a stronger flavor.

ron's rich, **DEEPLY SATISFYING** dipping SAUCE

(WITH ACKNOWLEDGMENTS TO THE BARON OF BARBECUE, PAUL KIRK)

Makes about 6 cups | 1.5 L

Any student of barbecue has to bow in the direction of Kansas City once in a while, and Paul Kirk is one of the world's greatest barbecue cooks and also perhaps its best-known ambassador. Paul has taught thousands of cooks the essentials of barbecue, and this rich, sweet, tangy sauce is based on his Kansas City classic.

2 Tbsp | 25 mL powdered ancho, poblano or New Mexico chile

1 Tbsp | 15 mL ground black pepper

1 Tbsp | 15 mL dry mustard

1 tsp | 5 mL ground coriander

1 tsp | 5 mL ground allspice

1/4 tsp | 1 mL ground cloves

1/2 tsp | 2 mL grated nutmeg

up to 1 tsp | 5 mL cayenne pepper, according to your taste

1/4 cup | 50 mL neutral-flavored oil

1 onion, finely chopped

6 cloves garlic, finely chopped

1 shallot, minced

1/2 cup | 125 mL tightly packed dark brown sugar

1 cup | 250 mL white vinegar

1/2 cup | 125 mL clover honey

1/4 cup | 50 mL Worcestershire sauce or soy sauce or a combination

1 tsp | 5 mL liquid smoke or hickory-smoked salt (optional)

32-oz | 1-L keg Heinz ketchup

Mix all the spices together and set aside. Heat the oil in a big pot over medium heat and gently sauté the onion, garlic and shallot until tender. Add the spices and mix thoroughly, cooking for 2 or 3 minutes to bring out their flavors. Add the remaining ingredients and simmer the mixture for 30 minutes, stirring often (be careful, it spatters). Don't cook too long or it will start to caramelize and you'll have spicy fudge. If you want a very smooth sauce, blend with a hand blender or food processor. Preserve as you would a jam or jelly in mason jars. Use as a glaze or a dip for barbecued meats, or as a flavoring sauce in fajitas.

NOTE: This thick sauce is designed for dipping. If you want to use it as a baste or a glaze, thin it with water, apple juice or Jack Daniel's to suit your taste and the task at hand.

PLANKING
⤚ SECRET ⤙

Use sauce sparingly when plank-cooking meat. In barbecue competitions we use it only as a finishing glaze. If you baste meat with a sugary sauce too early, it will turn black when the sugar caramelizes from the heat. Also use sauce sparingly when you serve, offering it to guests on the side. Too much sauce and you lose the smoky flavor you've worked so hard to achieve!

classic mustard-BASED BARBECUE sauce

Makes about 2 cups | 500 mL

Who knows why most barbecue sauces are sweet and tomato-based? This tangy, mustardy sauce is very much alive in the Carolinas and Georgia, but almost unheard-of in most other places.

It's delicious, of course, with pork.

2 Tbsp | 25 mL vegetable oil

1 medium onion, finely minced

4 cloves garlic, finely minced

1 cup | 250 mL cider vinegar

2/3 cup | 150 mL prepared mustard

1/3 cup | 75 mL brown sugar

1 Tbsp | 15 mL ancho chile powder

1 Tbsp | 15 mL paprika

1 tsp | 5 mL finely ground black pepper

1/4 tsp | 1 mL cayenne pepper

2 Tbsp | 25 mL butter or margarine

dash soy sauce or Worcestershire sauce

Over low to medium heat, heat the vegetable oil, add the onion and garlic and sauté until soft but not browned. Add the vinegar, mustard, sugar, chile powder, paprika, black pepper and cayenne pepper. Bring to a boil and simmer for 10 minutes. Stir in the butter or margarine and soy or Worcestershire sauce and remove from the heat. If you prefer a smoother sauce to one with little chunks of onion and garlic, purée with a hand blender before serving. This sauce is good warm, but it stores indefinitely in the fridge.

asian BARBECUE sauce

Makes about 2¹/₂ cups | 625 mL

This is great as a marinade and a basting sauce for ribs and steaks, but is also good with chicken and firm-fleshed fish. Be careful—its strong flavors can overwhelm what you're cooking. Marinate for a maximum of 4 hours for meat and 1 hour for chicken and fish.

one 12-ounce | 355-mL bottle hoisin sauce

1/2 cup | 125 mL light soy sauce

2 Tbsp | 25 mL sherry vinegar

juice of 1 orange

1/2 cup | 125 mL plum sauce

1/2 Tbsp | 7 mL five-spice powder

2 Tbsp | 25 mL toasted sesame oil

2 Tbsp | 25 mL oyster sauce

2 shallots, finely minced

2 Tbsp | 25 mL finely minced garlic

2 Tbsp | 25 mL finely minced fresh ginger

2 Tbsp | 25 mL honey

1 Tbsp | 15 mL finely chopped chives or green onion

Mix all the ingredients together in a nonreactive bowl. Use soon after making; it won't keep more than a few days in the fridge.

flavored BUTTERS for all OCCASIONS

Once you've made any of these savoury butters you'll always want to keep some in the freezer. Brought to room temperature, they're incredible on roasted corn on the cob or slathered on cornbread, and a pat of flavored butter on a freshly grilled steak or fish fillet is heavenly. You can even use it as a sautéing butter for thinly sliced mushrooms or scrambled eggs, or toss with some cooked noodles for a quick, easy side.

Mediterranean Butter

4 Tbsp | 50 mL finely chopped flat-leaf Italian parsley

4 Tbsp | 50 mL finely chopped combination of fresh dill, basil or mint (or any combination of fresh herbs—try chervil, tarragon, sage, rosemary, etc.)

1 lb | 500 g unsalted butter, at room temperature

kosher salt to taste

Red Pepper Butter

1 red bell pepper, roasted, peeled, seeded and coarsely chopped

1/2 lb | 250 g unsalted butter, at room temperature

1 tsp | 5 mL sweet paprika

kosher salt to taste

Garlic Chive Butter

4 cloves garlic, put through a garlic press
(or 8 cloves roasted garlic, squeezed out of their skins)

2 Tbsp | 25 mL finely chopped fresh chives

1/2 lb | 250 g unsalted butter, at room temperature

kosher salt to taste

Gorgonzola Butter

3/4 cup | 175 mL Gorgonzola cheese

**1/4 lb | 125 g unsalted butter at
room temperature**

1 tsp | 5 mL fresh lemon juice

kosher salt to taste

Cut the butter into cubes and place in a food processor. Add the flavoring ingredients and whiz until thoroughly blended. If you're serving it right away with corn, or on a piece of grilled meat, just place in a small bowl and serve.

If you want to store it, use a spatula to transfer the butter onto a sheet of waxed paper or plastic wrap and shape it into a rough cylinder. Fold the wrap around the butter and shape it into an even cylinder about $1^1/2$ inches | 4 cm in diameter. Twist the ends so the tube is sealed and tight, and fasten both ends with a twist-tie. Refrigerate or freeze until you need it. To serve, slice off disks of butter to dress steaks or corn, or to stuff inside a burger.

Roasted
➤ Garlic ≈

Here's a great kitchen staple that works well baked in the oven or planked on the grill. Roasted garlic is as versatile as it is delicious. Use it as a flavor enhancer in mayo, an enricher of mashed potatoes and a flavor note in soups and sauces—or just spread it on a piece of toasted French bread.

Preheat the oven to 350°F | 175°C (or preheat your grill in preparation for plank-cooking). With a sharp knife, slice off the top of a garlic bulb, just enough to expose the tops of the cloves. Drizzle with a little olive oil, season with salt and pepper and wrap the bulb tightly in foil. Place in the oven (or on a plank in your grill with the heat turned down to low), cut side up, and roast for about an hour, or until the garlic is soft and lightly browned. Once it's cool enough to handle, you can squeeze the head and the roasted garlic comes out like toothpaste.

EASIEST, TASTIEST steak (OR ANYTHING ELSE) MARINADE

Makes about 1¹/₂ cups | 375 mL, enough for 4 to 6 steaks

I use this mainly as a quick and delicious marinade for beefsteak, but it's also great with pork chops or chicken, as well as rich, meaty fish like salmon, halibut, tuna and swordfish. I've provided precise measures of the ingredients, but it's really meant to be a marinade that you just throw together. A few glugs of soy sauce, a small glug of sesame oil, as much garlic and ginger as you like, and so on. Once you try this, it will become a standard in your kitchen.

1 cup | 250 mL dark soy sauce

1 tsp | 5 mL toasted sesame oil

2 cloves garlic, finely minced

1 Tbsp | 15 mL finely chopped or grated fresh ginger

freshly ground black pepper

**juice of 1/2 lemon or 1/4 cup | 50 mL mirin
(Japanese sweet rice wine)**

1 Tbsp | 15 mL tapioca starch (cornstarch will also do)

Mix the soy sauce, sesame oil, garlic, ginger, black pepper, lemon juice or mirin and tapioca starch in a nonreactive baking dish. Add the meat or fish, turn to coat, and marinate for 10 minutes to 1/2 hour, turning once or twice. Don't marinate overnight, as this is a fairly salty marinade.

doctored MAYONNAISE

I love plain old mayo—in sandwiches, as a dip for french fries, as a simple dressing for hot or cold veggies. But mix in some extra flavor and you've got something that sends your taste buds to new heights. These variations are my favorites, but feel free to create your own.

The technique is simple: combine good-quality store-bought mayonnaise with the other ingredients in a food processor and whiz until they're smooth, then refrigerate. If possible, store for a day, or at least a few hours, to let the flavors marry and intensify.

Margie's Chipotle and Roasted Garlic Mayo

This invention of Calgary caterer Margie Gibb is particularly good as a dip for pieces of smoked or grilled sausage, but it's also great on just about anything.

1¹/₂ cups | 375 mL mayonnaise

1 whole head roasted garlic, cloves squeezed
out of their skins

1 tsp | 5 mL finely ground cumin (preferably made
from toasted cumin seeds)

1 Tbsp | 15 mL chopped chipotles in adobo sauce
(add more of the chipotles if you like it hot)

Sesame Mayo

This is the perfect dip for roasted veggies, and it's also great tossed with rice noodles for a cool, creamy side to grilled Asian-flavored meats. Sprinkle with toasted sesame seeds for extra texture.

1 cup | 250 mL mayonnaise

1 tsp | 5 mL toasted sesame oil

1/2 tsp | 2 mL soy sauce (or to taste)

1 tsp | 5 mL Chinese chili sauce or
spicy Szechuan chili oil (or to taste)

1 tsp | 5 mL grated or finely chopped
fresh lemon, lime or orange rind

1 to 2 Tbsp | 25 mL toasted sesame seeds (to taste)

continues on next page ...

Curry Mayo

This is perfect with veggies or as a sandwich spread.

2 large shallots, peeled and finely chopped

4 tsp | 20 mL curry powder

1 Tbsp | 15 mL vegetable oil

1 cup | 250 mL mayonnaise

juice of 1/2 lemon

Barbecue Mayo

A great "secret sauce" for your homemade burger, french fries or grilled chicken wings. Cut it with sour cream for a tasty chip dip.

1 Tbsp | 15 mL barbecue rub of your choice

1/4 cup | 50 mL barbecue sauce of your choice

1 cup | 250 mL mayonnaise

lemon or lime juice

Wasabi Mayo

Excellent on planked fish, or on fried crab cakes, or in a slaw or salad.

1 Tbsp | 15 mL wasabi powder or paste

1 cup | 250 mL mayonnaise

juice of 1 lime

Balsamic Reduction

In *Barbecue Secrets*, balsamic reduction is used to finish grilled rack of lamb. But this incredible, tangy, sweet, rich syrup has a multitude of uses. It supercharges any vinaigrette. It's great in marinades (or as a simple marinade on its own), and you can even drizzle it on ice cream or fruit.

Pour a 10-oz | 300-mL bottle of cheap balsamic vinegar (you could use more or less as your need dictates; this is just a handy amount to prepare) in a small saucepan and bring to a boil over medium-high heat. Cook at a gently rolling boil, watching carefully, until the vinegar has reduced to about 1/3 its original volume (about 10 to 15 minutes). When it's ready, it should be a thick syrup that coats the back of a spoon. Set aside to cool. Transfer to a squeeze bottle and store it in a cool dry place. It keeps indefinitely.

PEACH and BLACKBERRY salsa

Serves 4

This is something you should try only when these fruits are at their peak, which on the west coast of Canada is in August. Paired with planked chicken, this one's a mind-blower.

4 peaches, peeled and diced, not too small

**1 cup | 250 mL fresh blackberries,
washed and picked over**

1/4 cup | 50 mL red onion, diced

**1/2 fresh green jalapeño or other hot pepper,
seeded and minced**

juice of 2 limes

salt and freshly ground black pepper

In a bowl, combine all the ingredients. Let the salsa stand, covered, in the fridge for about an hour.

MANGO AND STRAWBERRY salsa

Serves 4

The tartness of the mango and the sweetness of the strawberries make for a stirring salsa. Serve this with marinated flank steak in a fajita or as a garnish with barbecued beef or spicy pork. You might even like the leftovers on your morning yogurt.

3 mangoes

1 cup | 250 mL fresh strawberries, preferably local

1/4 cup | 50 mL diced red onion

1/2 hot pepper, seeded and minced, or to taste

juice of 1 lime

1 Tbsp | 15 mL chopped cilantro

kosher salt and freshly ground black pepper

In a bowl, combine all the ingredients. Let the salsa stand, covered, in the fridge for about an hour.

STARTERS AND SIDES

Chapter 3

**an** cannot live by plank alone. In fact, your guests will start to lose patience when absolutely everything you're serving them has a smoky flavor. Because cooking, like life, is all about balance, I'm providing two sections of appetizers and sides: the first a collection of planked dishes and the second a short compendium of recipes that complement planked food precisely because they don't taste like smoke.

PLANKETIZERS AND SIDEBOARDS

There's almost no limit to what you can cook on a plank. Here's a collection of classic and quirky dishes that are guaranteed to raise an eyebrow or two. In a good way.

cheesy GARLIC BREAD

Serves 6 as an appetizer

I guess this is the closest I'll ever get to a wood-fired bread oven. Get the plank going and make these in batches, because they're going to disappear fast.

1 fruitwood or alder plank, soaked overnight or at least 1 hour

2 cloves garlic, smashed or pushed through a garlic press

1/2 cup | 125 mL extra virgin olive oil

1 loaf French bread, sliced at an angle for longer pieces

1/2 lb | 250 g finely grated Asiago cheese

1/4 lb | 125 g finely grated Parmigiano-Reggiano cheese

finely chopped green onions or chives for garnish

chopped fresh tomatoes with olive oil and fresh chopped basil for garnish

1 part balsamic vinegar and 2 parts extra virgin olive oil for dipping

In a bowl combine the garlic and olive oil. Prepare the bread slices by brushing them with the garlic oil. Place a layer of grated Asiago on each slice, and then sprinkle some Parmigiano-Reggiano on top.

Preheat the grill on medium-high for 5 or 10 minutes or until the chamber temperature rises above 500°F | 260°C. Rinse the plank and place it on the cooking grate. Cover the grill and heat the plank for 4 or 5 minutes, or until it starts to throw off a bit of smoke and crackles lightly. Reduce the heat to medium. Put the bread slices, cheese side up, of course, on the plank. Cook until the cheese is melted. Serve with the garnishes, or just as it comes out of the grill.

planked **chicken** SATAY

Makes 24 appetizer-sized portions

Satay is one of the great finger foods. I recommend using hardwood planks for these to complement their sweetness. Because they're not grilled over direct heat, they won't char like traditional satay, but they make up for it with their smoky flavor.

NOTE: It's hard to lay 24 skewers on 2 planks and leave enough room for heat to circulate around the meat, so I've invented a crazy technique that will allow you to cook all 24 on one plank. Check it out at the end of this recipe.

2 hardwood planks, soaked overnight or at least 1 hour

twenty-four 7-inch | 18-cm bamboo skewers, soaked in water for 15 to 30 minutes

For the peanut sauce:

half of a 14-oz | 398-mL can unsweetened coconut milk

1/3 cup | 75 mL chunky-style peanut butter

1 garlic clove, chopped

2 Tbsp | 25 mL soy sauce

1 Tbsp | 15 mL light brown sugar

pinch cayenne pepper

1 tsp | 5 mL Thai fish sauce (optional)

For the chicken:

the other half of a 14-oz | 398-mL can unsweetened coconut milk

2 tsp | 10 mL fresh ginger, finely minced

2 tsp | 10 mL curry powder

1 tsp | 5 mL ground coriander

2 Tbsp | 25 mL light brown sugar

Juice of 1 lime

2 Tbsp | 25 mL Thai fish sauce (optional)

3 boneless, skinless chicken breasts (about 1¼ lb | 625 g)

Make the peanut sauce by combining all the ingredients in a food processor and whizzing them until just combined (too long and you lose the crunch of the crunchy peanut butter). Transfer to a bowl and refrigerate. This can be made several days in advance.

Split the chicken breasts horizontally into thin, flat slabs. Cut the slabs into 3-inch by 1-inch strips (7.5 cm by 2.5 cm). Combine the remaining ingredients in a nonreactive bowl, mixing well to dissolve the sugar.

Add the chicken to the marinade, stirring to coat. Cover and refrigerate for 2 hours or up to 24 hours.

Thread the chicken onto the skewers, one strip per skewer. Preheat the grill on medium-high for 5 or 10 minutes or until the chamber temperature rises above 500°F | 260°C. Rinse the planks and place them on the cooking grate. Cover the grill and heat the planks for 4 or 5 minutes, or until they start to throw off a bit of smoke and crackle lightly. Reduce the heat to medium. Place the satay skewers on the planks, leaving a little room between each for circulation. Cook for 3 to 5 minutes, turning once or twice and making sure to put out any flare-ups with a spray bottle.

Transfer the satay to a platter and serve with the peanut sauce.

Try this crazy technque if you dare!

stuffed MUSHROOMS

Makes 24 hors d'oeuvres

This classic stuffed mushroom recipe, adapted from an old *Gourmet* magazine, is wonderful on a plank.

2 planks (any kind will do), soaked overnight or at least 1 hour

24 large button mushrooms (about 2^1/$_2$ lb | 1.25 kg)

12 oz | 375 g sun-dried tomatoes packed in oil, drained, reserving 4 Tbsp| 50 mL of the oil

1/3 cup | 75 mL finely chopped shallot

1 tsp | 5 mL finely chopped garlic

pinch crumbled dried thyme

kosher salt and freshly ground black pepper

3 Tbsp | 45 mL heavy cream

1/4 cup | 50 mL freshly grated Parmesan

Remove the stems from the mushrooms and finely chop 1 cup | 250 mL of the stems, discarding the rest. Mince the tomatoes. Brush the mushroom caps with some of the reserved tomato oil and arrange them on a baking sheet, stemmed sides up. In a large skillet over low-medium heat, cook the shallot and garlic in the remaining tomato oil, stirring occasionally, until they're softened. Stir in the reserved mushroom stems, minced tomatoes, thyme, salt and pepper. Cook the mixture, stirring occasionally, for 5 to 10 minutes, or until the liquid has evaporated and the mixture is thick. Stir in the cream, divide the mixture among the mushroom caps, and sprinkle them with the Parmesan.

Preheat the grill on medium-high for 5 or 10 minutes or until the chamber temperature rises above 500°F | 260°C. Rinse the planks and place them on the cooking grate. Cover the grill and heat the planks for 4 or 5 minutes, or until they start to throw off a bit of smoke and crackle lightly. Reduce the heat to medium-low. Quickly and carefully place the mushrooms on the planks. Cook for 10 to 15 minutes, or until the filling has heated through.

PLANKED MUSHROOMS or VEGGIE kebabs
WITH TARRAGON VINAIGRETTE

Serves 4 as an appetizer

This is a great way to add some smoky flavor to veggies. The first time I cooked this recipe, I just piled the dressed mushrooms on a plank, but you can use the same treatment with your favorite veggies on skewers. This dish is great right off the plank as a hot appetizer, or cooled and served as part of an appetizer platter.

1 cedar plank, soaked overnight or at least 1 hour

6 or 8 bamboo skewers, soaked for at least 15 minutes

1/2 cup | 125 mL extra virgin olive oil

3 Tbsp | 45 mL white wine vinegar or tarragon vinegar

1 Tbsp | 15 mL Dijon mustard

1 shallot, finely chopped

1 clove garlic, smashed or finely minced

1 tsp | 5 mL dried crumbled tarragon leaves

juice of 1/2 lemon

kosher salt and freshly ground black pepper

24 large white button mushrooms (or 24 bite-sized chunks of mixed vegetables, including red onion, zucchini, Japanese eggplant, red, green or yellow bell peppers, cherry tomatoes, etc.)

Preheat the grill on medium-high for 5 or 10 minutes, or until the chamber temperature rises above 500°F | 260°C. Rinse the plank and place it on the cooking grate. Cover the grill and heat the plank for 4 or 5 minutes, or until it starts to throw off a bit of smoke and crackles lightly. While the plank is preheating, whisk together the olive oil, vinegar, mustard, shallot, garlic, tarragon and lemon juice. Season the vinaigrette to taste with salt and pepper.

Toss the mushrooms or veggies in the vinaigrette. If you're making kebabs, place the veggies on the skewers. Place on the plank and leave the heat on medium-high. Cook for 6 to 8 minutes or until the vegetables are heated through and starting to brown around the edges. Remove from the heat and transfer to a serving dish. Squeeze more lemon over the mushrooms and season them with more salt and pepper, if you like.

PLANKED **brie** with roasted **tomato** AND **CHERRY RELISH**

Serves 8 to 12

I know. Just the name of the recipe sounds luscious. And it is. Roasting the cherries and tomatoes takes a while, but there's no heavy lifting involved, and planking the cheese is a snap. One taste of this molten, smoky, tangy/sweet concoction and you'll be addicted. I want to acknowledge my friend Gail Norton for the relish recipe, and planking god Ted Reader for the cooking technique, which he showcases in his great book, the *Sticks & Stones* cookbook. I've also provided an alternative topping, caramelized onions, which are great with almost anything.

1 maple or fruitwood plank, soaked overnight or at least 1 hour

2 small rounds brie (1/4 lb | 125 g each)

1 cup | 250 mL Roasted Tomato-Cherry Relish (recipe follows)

2 Tbsp | 15 mL balsamic reduction (see sidebar page 46)

Preheat the grill on medium-high for 5 or 10 minutes or until the chamber temperature rises above 500°F | 260°C.

Cut the top of the rind off each of the rounds of brie. Grind a little pepper over the exposed cheese. Spread about 1/2 cup | 125 mL of the relish over the brie rounds.

Rinse the plank and place it on the cooking grate. Cover the grill and heat the plank for 4 or 5 minutes, or until it starts to throw off a bit of smoke and crackles lightly. Place the cheese on the plank and cook for 10 to 12 minutes, or until the cheese turns golden and starts to soften (be careful not to overcook—the cheese can fall apart, and then you've got a tasty mess on your hands). Remove from the grill and drizzle with the balsamic reduction. Garnish with a few fresh grape tomatoes and/or cherries and serve, on the plank, with crusty bread, rye crisps or your favorite crackers.

Roasted Tomato-Cherry Relish

Makes about 2 cups | 500 mL

1 lb | 500 g ripe fresh cherries, pits removed

1 lb | 500 g grape tomatoes or small cherry tomatoes

1/4 cup | 50 mL extra virgin olive oil

1 tsp | 5 mL kosher salt

balsamic reduction for drizzling (see sidebar page 46)

Preheat the oven to 350°F | 180°C. Spread the cherries and tomatoes on a large baking pan in one layer. Drizzle the oil and sprinkle the salt over the fruit and toss to coat. Place in the oven and roast for 1 hour, mixing them around once or twice. Reduce the heat to 300°F | 150°C and roast for another hour, again mixing once or twice. The tomatoes and cherries should be nicely caramelized. Drizzle with a little more oil and a splash of balsamic vinegar, mix thoroughly and transfer to a storage container. This relish keeps in the fridge for 1 or 2 weeks and freezes well.

Caramelized Onions

Makes about 1 cup | 250 mL

This makes a great topping for burgers and is an excellent all-purpose condiment. Try it as an omelet filling or a topping for grilled pork chops. Mix it with goat cheese and spread it on crackers for a tangy sweet appetizer.

2 Tbsp | 25 mL butter, olive oil or a combination of both

4 medium onions, peeled and sliced into rings

1/2 tsp | 2 mL kosher salt

1 tsp | 5 mL sugar

1/2 tsp | 2 mL ground cinnamon

pinch cayenne

In a large skillet heat the butter/olive oil over medium heat. Add the onion rings and salt and sauté until soft, about 5 minutes. Add the sugar, cinnamon and cayenne and continue to sauté, stirring regularly, until the onions are shiny and brown, being careful not to burn them (add a little water if necessary to prevent burning).

PLANKED curried cashews

Makes 4 cups | 1 L

My wife Kate's curried cashews are a staple at Christmas. They're the perfect bread-and-butter gift to bring to parties and they're excellent with festive cocktails. Nothing enhances the rye-and-ginger or bourbon-and-Coke experience like this. Kate's grandmother Mimi tasted these delicious nuts and quickly instructed us to start a business selling them. "You can call it Kath-Ron Nuts for Cocktails," she said with matronly enthusiasm. Pretty catchy, eh? NOT!

**1 hardwood (maple, hickory, oak or apple)
cooking plank, soaked overnight or at least 1 hour**

2 lb | 1 kg raw unsalted cashews

1/4 lb | 125 g butter

1 Tbsp | 15 mL kosher salt

1 tsp | 5 mL sugar

1 Tbsp | 15 mL curry powder

Preheat the grill on medium-high for 5 or 10 minutes or until the chamber temperature rises above 500°F | 260°C. Rinse the plank and place it on the cooking grate. Cover the grill and heat the plank for 4 or 5 minutes, or until it starts to throw off a bit of smoke and crackles lightly. Reduce the heat to medium-low. Place a disposable foil pie plate on the plank and spread the cashews in the plate. Cover the grill and cook for 5 to 10 minutes, turning frequently, or until the nuts turn golden brown. Transfer the nuts to a bowl. If all the nuts don't fit in the pie plate, grill them in batches, keeping the heat low and taking care to minimize flare-ups with a spray bottle.

In a skillet, melt the butter over medium heat and toss in the cashews. Sprinkle in half the salt, sugar and curry powder and stir to coat. Transfer to a paper towel, and while the nuts are still hot, add the rest of the ingredients and mix to coat. If any are left by the time they cool, package in an airtight container and store in a cool, dry place. They also freeze well.

cedar-**brie**
PLANKED WITH GRILLED PINEAPPLE TOPPING

Serves 8 to 12

This recipe, first featured in Ted Reader's *On Fire in the Kitchen*, is a classic fave from the King of the Q—rich, flashy and outrageously delicious. I love his words about the topping: "Be sure to load it on." Go, Teddy, go!

1 cedar plank, soaked overnight or at least 1 hour

three 1/2-inch-thick | 1-cm slices ripe pineapple

2 Tbsp | 25 mL vegetable oil

1 jalapeño pepper, finely chopped

3 shallots, thinly sliced

**1/2 cup | 125 mL pineapple marmalade or
orange marmalade**

1/4 cup | 50 mL white wine

2 green onions, thinly sliced

1 Tbsp | 15 mL chopped fresh thyme

kosher salt and freshly ground black pepper

2 Brie wheels (each 1/2 lb | 250 g)

Preheat the grill to high. Grill the pineapple slices for 2 to 3 minutes per side or until lightly charred. Set aside to cool. Coarsely chop the pineapple and set aside.

Heat the vegetable oil in a medium saucepan over medium-high heat. Sauté the jalapeño and shallots for 1 to 2 minutes, until tender. Add the marmalade and wine, stirring until the marmalade becomes liquid. Remove from the heat and stir in the grilled pineapple, green onions and thyme. Season with salt and pepper. Let cool completely.

Rinse the plank and evenly space the Brie wheels on it. Top each piece of Brie with the pineapple mixture, being sure to load it on. Place the planked Brie on the grill and close the lid. Bake for 5 minutes. Carefully open the lid; if the plank is on fire, spray it with water and reduce the heat to medium. Close the lid and continue to cook for 8 to 10 minutes, until the Brie is golden brown, soft and beginning to bulge. Be careful not to let the cheese burst—the insides will ooze out and you'll lose all the precious and decadent ooey, gooey cheese. Serve immediately on the plank with lots of bread and crackers.

THE BARON'S PLANKED sweet HICKORY bacon bites

Serves 20

This recipe comes from one of my mentors and one of the world's best-known barbecue cooks, Chef Paul Kirk. "I don't think that people realize cooking on planks can give food a new and wonderful change from everyday BBQ," says Paul.

1 hickory plank (or plank of your choice), soaked in water or apple juice for at least 1 hour

20 water-soaked toothpicks

20 whole roasted, unsalted pecan halves or almonds

20 pitted prunes, dates or figs

10 slices bacon, cut in half

Stuff 1 whole pecan half or almond in each prune, date or fig. Wrap a piece of bacon around the fruit and secure with a toothpick. (When you get to the nut meat, twist or screw the toothpick; this will keep the nuts from breaking.) Place the bites on a prepared plank. Cook at 350° to 425° F | 180° to 222° C for 18 to 25 minutes. Add soaked hickory chips to your hot coals or over your grill burner for more hickory flavor, if you want.

plank-ROASTED RED PEPPER soup

Serves 6

This soup has been a staple in our house for many years. The wonderful flavor of roasted peppers is delivered to the taste buds in a velvety concoction that's great hot or cold. It's based on a Cuban recipe from Taunton's *Fine Cooking* magazine.

**1 hardwood plank (fruitwood would work best),
soaked overnight or at least 1 hour**

5 red bell peppers

1 Tbsp | 15 mL extra virgin olive oil

1/2 medium onion, finely chopped

2 cloves garlic, finely chopped

pinch cayenne pepper

3$^1/_2$ cups | 875 mL chicken stock

kosher salt and freshly ground black pepper

**sour cream, diced onion and parsley or
cilantro sprigs for garnish**

Preheat the grill on medium-high for 5 or 10 minutes or until the chamber temperature rises above 500°F | 260°C. Rinse the plank and place it on the cooking grate. Cover the grill and heat the plank for 4 or 5 minutes, or until it starts to throw off a bit of smoke and crackles lightly. Keep the heat at medium-high and place the bell peppers on the plank. Roast for 20 to 25 minutes, turning regularly, until the skins are evenly blackened. (This is one case where flare-ups accelerate and enhance the roasting process.) Remove the blackened peppers from the grill and place in a nonreactive bowl. Cover the bowl to let the peppers steam as they cool. When the peppers are cool enough to handle, peel off the skins and remove the seeds and stems. Don't rinse them or you'll lose their essential oils.

Purée the roasted red peppers in a food processor and set aside.

Heat the oil in a large pot and cook the onion and garlic over medium-high heat until soft and translucent. Add the puréed peppers, cayenne and chicken stock, stirring to combine. Season with salt and pepper and simmer for 10 minutes. Serve the soup in bowls with a dollop of sour cream, garnished with diced onion and a sprig of parsley or cilantro.

GAZPACHO with plank-smoked tomatoes

I introduced smoked tomatoes to backyard cook Lawrence Davis at one of my cooking classes, and he developed this recipe to showcase them in a classic gazpacho, Spanish for refreshing, cold summer soup. The recipe serves 8, but Lawrence says it can be doubled or tripled for a large crowd. For extra flavor and variety add corn, Greek olives, or any seasonal vegetable, coarsely chopped. You can also serve some chopped hard-boiled egg or crumbled bacon on the side for guests to add at the table.

1 maple, hickory, oak or mesquite plank,
soaked overnight or at least 1 hour

4 large, ripe, firm tomatoes

1 long English cucumber

1 green bell pepper

1 yellow bell pepper

2 medium onions

2 stalks celery

6 cups | 1.5 L tomato juice

2/3 cup | 150 mL extra virgin olive oil

1/3 cup | 75 mL balsamic vinegar

juice of 1 lemon

dried or fresh herbs, such as rosemary, thyme and
basil, to taste (if you use dried, don't use too much
or you'll add a bitter taste to the soup)

kosher salt and freshly ground black pepper

Worcestershire sauce

Louisiana-style hot pepper sauce

Preheat the grill on medium-high for 5 or 10 minutes or until the chamber temperature rises above 500°F | 260°C. Rinse the plank and place it on the cooking grate. Cover the grill and heat the plank for 4 or 5 minutes, or until it starts to throw off a bit of smoke and crackles lightly. (You may want to put a brick on the plank as it's preheating. This will prevent warping so your tomatoes don't roll off the plank.) Reduce the heat to low, place the whole, unpeeled tomatoes on the plank, cover and cook for 15 to 30 minutes, depending how smoky and soft you want the tomatoes. The skins will split and take on a yellowish cast from the smoke.

Remove the tomatoes from the plank, peel and coarsely chop. Prepare and coarsely chop the remaining vegetables; combine with the tomatoes in a large bowl. Pour in the tomato juice, olive oil, vinegar and lemon juice. Season with herbs, salt, pepper, Worcestershire sauce and hot pepper sauce to suit your taste. Refrigerate several hours or overnight to allow the flavors to meld. (Taste after several hours and add more seasoning if needed.)

Serve in bowls or mugs taken straight from the freezer. Have the Worcestershire and hot sauce on hand for those who want to spice it up!

PLANKING
↣ SECRET ↢

Lightly smoked tomatoes are great in guacamole or gazpacho, and smokier and softer tomatoes are wonderful in soups, stews and sauces.

PLANKED CALAMARI WITH FRESH tomato basil salsa

Serves 4

The secret to great squid is to use the freshest and smallest you can find, and to plank it over high heat for no more than 2 or 3 minutes. Any longer and it turns rubbery. In this recipe, the tomato salsa provides a cool, tangy, herbal complement to the hot, garlicky calamari. Great with a crisp, fruity white wine.

1 cedar plank, soaked overnight or at least 1 hour

**1 lb | 500 g cleaned squid, equal parts bodies
and tentacles (squid rings also work fine)**

1 Tbsp | 15 mL kosher salt

1/2 cup | 125 mL extra virgin olive oil

1/2 tsp | 2 mL red pepper flakes

2 cloves garlic, finely chopped

2 cups | 500 mL small, ripe cherry or grape tomatoes

1 Tbsp | 15 mL finely chopped fresh basil

1 Tbsp | 15 mL rice vinegar or white wine vinegar

salt and freshly ground black pepper

Coat the squid with the salt, then rinse thoroughly with cold water. Pat dry with paper towels. Slit the bodies and score the inside surface with diagonal cuts. Cut into large bite-sized pieces. Place in a bowl with 1/4 cup | 50 mL of the olive oil, the red pepper flakes and the garlic. Toss to coat and marinate for about an hour.

Preheat the grill on high for 5 minutes.

While the grill is heating, coarsely chop the tomatoes (halves or quarters are fine). Toss the tomatoes and basil in a bowl with the vinegar and the remaining olive oil and. Distribute the salsa among 4 plates.

Rinse the plank and place it on the cooking grate. Cover the grill and heat the plank for 4 or 5 minutes, or until it starts to throw off a bit of smoke and crackles lightly. Don't reduce the heat (as I usually instruct) because your cooking time with this recipe is so short. Also, don't worry too much about small flare-ups because they'll help sear the squid a little.

When the plank is ready, open the grill and quickly place the calamari on the plank. Cover the grill but don't walk away. After about a minute, open the grill and turn the squid. Close the grill and stand there for another minute or two. Check the squid, and taste one to make sure it's cooked through. Remove the squid from the grill and transfer to the plates. Sprinkle each serving with just a pinch of kosher salt and a light grinding of pepper. Drizzle with a little more olive oil and serve immediately.

PLANKED **scallops**

Serves 4

The sweet flavor and meaty texture of scallops is excellent with a little wood smoke. Food stylist Nathan Fong, who helped make my recipes look gorgeous for this book, came up with this recipe when I asked him how we should present the scallops for one of the color photos for the book. They look great, and they taste fantastic. Thanks for going above and beyond the call of duty, Nathan!

1 cooking plank (cedar is great, but any kind will do), soaked overnight or at least 1 hour

12 large or 16 medium-sized scallops

kosher salt

juice of 1/2 lemon

1 tsp | 5 mL finely grated lemon zest

1 Tbsp | 15 mL sherry vinegar

2 Tbsp | 25 mL butter

1 tsp | 5 mL chopped fresh dill

1/2 tsp | 2 mL crushed dried red chile flakes

1 Tbsp | 15 mL liquid honey

butter lettuce leaves

Garden Salsa (page 78)

lemon wedges and dill sprigs for garnish

Place the scallops in a nonreactive bowl. Season them with a little salt and set aside. In a saucepan over low heat, combine the lemon juice and zest, vinegar, butter, chopped dill, chile flakes and honey. Cook, stirring constantly, just until the butter is incorporated into the sauce. Remove from the heat and pour half the mixture over the scallops, tossing to coat.

Preheat the grill on medium-high for 5 or 10 minutes or until the chamber temperature rises above 500°F | 260°C. Rinse the plank and place it on the cooking grate. Cover the grill and heat the plank for 4 or 5 minutes, or until it starts to throw off a bit of smoke and crackles lightly. Keep the heat on medium-high.

Place the scallops on the plank, cover the grill and cook for 2 to 3 minutes. Turn and baste the scallops and cook for another minute or until they're almost done. If you like a little charring, you can move the scallops onto the cooking grate for the last 1 or 2 minutes of cooking.

Remove the scallops from the grill and toss with the rest of the basting sauce. Serve on a leaf of butter lettuce garnished with a lemon wedge, a sprig of dill and a spoonful of Garden Salsa.

PLANKED
asparagus & prosciutto BUNDLES

Serves 6

These are a favorite of my brother Allan, who, like me, is a Ukrainian boy somehow transformed into a lover of all things Italian. This classic combination of flavors takes well to the plank and works as an appetizer, a side or on top of a salad. If you can't find real imported fontina, use Parmigiano-Reggiano shaved into slivers. You really don't want a flavorless cheese here.

1 plank, soaked overnight or at least 1 hour

18 choice, thick asparagus spears

1/2 lb | 250 g Italian fontina cheese, cut into thin slices

6 large slices prosciutto

1 Tbsp | 15 mL butter

balsamic reduction (optional) (see sidebar page 46)

crusty bread as accompaniment

Trim and blanch the asparagus in salted water for just a minute or two until it's deep green and still firm. Stop the cooking by immersing the spears in cold water.

Set aside 12 slices of cheese. Use the rest of the cheese to place on top of the rolls as described below. Spread open a slice of prosciutto and place 3 spears of asparagus on it. Place the cheese between the spears. Wrap the prosciutto around the spears. Proceed until you have 6 bundles.

Preheat the grill on medium-high for 5 or 10 minutes or until the chamber temperature rises above 500°F | 260°C. Rinse the plank and place it on the cooking grate. Cover the grill and heat the plank for 4 or 5 minutes, or until it starts to throw off a bit of smoke and crackles lightly. Reduce the heat to medium-low and place the bundles on the plank. Working quickly, place the remaining cheese slices over each bundle in a criss-cross pattern. Cook for 10 to 15 minutes or until the cheese is melted and a little mottled. Remove from the grill, drizzle with a little olive oil or brush with the butter, and let sit for a few minutes. Plate these individually with a few drops of balsamic reduction around the edges, if desired. Serve with crusty bread.

SCALLOP and CUCUMBER salad

Serves 6

This recipe is a little fancier than most, but it's so good I have to share it with you. It comes from Jenni Neidhart, a Calgary caterer I've had the pleasure of working with on occasion. It calls for Lebanese cucumbers (small, tender-skinned versions of long English cukes) as well as something called vanilla vinegar. What the heck is that, you say? So did I. It's champagne vinegar (which is available in gourmet food stores) infused with leftover vanilla pods for a month or more. So, when you cook any recipes from this book that call for vanilla beans, save the pods to make the vinegar in this recipe. Of course, the salad also tastes great with plain old champagne vinegar.

1 cooking plank, soaked overnight or for at least 1 hour

4 Lebanese cucumbers (or 1 small long English cucumber),
finely diced (leave the skin on)

1 red bell pepper, seeded and finely diced

1 yellow bell pepper, seeded and finely diced

1/2 red onion, finely diced

1 orange, zested and juiced

1 lemon, zested and juiced

1 lime, zested and juiced

1 jalapeño, seeds removed and finely diced

olive oil

vanilla vinegar (or champagne vinegar)

kosher salt and freshly ground pepper

1/4 cup | 50 mL fresh mint, finely chopped

12 large scallops

sesame sea salt (optional; make it by combining sea salt
and toasted sesame seeds in a mortar and pestle or food processor)

Combine cucumber, bell peppers and onion in a medium-sized bowl. Make a vinaigrette by mixing the juice and zest of all the citrus, jalapeño, a tiny bit of olive oil, vinegar and salt and pepper. Toss with the diced vegetables, and mix in the mint. Easy as that! Chill until serving time.

Preheat the grill on medium-high for 5 or 10 minutes or until the chamber temperature rises above 500°F | 260°C. Rinse the plank and place it on the cooking grate. Cover the grill and heat the plank for 4 or 5 minutes, or until it starts to throw off a bit of smoke and crackles lightly. Season the scallops with a little kosher salt and put them on the plank, keeping the heat on medium-high. Cover the grill and cook for 2 or 3 minutes, then turn and cook for another couple of minutes, until the scallops are springy to the touch.

Serve hot over the chilled cucumber salad and finish with a few drops of olive oil and a light sprinkle of sesame sea salt, if desired.

PLANK-baked STUFFED potatoes

Serves 5

These potatoes are baked in the oven and finished on a plank, which adds an extra dimension of smoky flavor that's brought out further if you use smoked Gouda instead of cheddar. (My kids thought the smoked Gouda version was too smoky, but I loved it.)

1 hardwood plank (alder, maple or oak works best here), soaked overnight or at least 1 hour

3 baking potatoes

1 Tbsp | 15 mL kosher salt (or even coarser salt like Malden or Fleur de Sel)

1/2 medium onion, chopped

2 cloves garlic, minced

1/4 cup | 50 mL butter

1/4 cup | 50 mL whipping cream

1/2 tsp | 2 mL freshly grated nutmeg

1 cup | 250 mL grated cheddar cheese (or smoked Gouda)

1/2 cup | 25 mLgrated Parmesan cheese

1 Tbsp | 15 mL olive oil

paprika

sour cream

chopped chives

Preheat the oven to 400°F | 200°C. Wash and scrub the potatoes under cold water and puncture the skin in a few places with a fork. While the potatoes are still damp, coat them generously with salt, reserving about 1 tsp | 5 mL for seasoning the filling later. Bake for about 1 hour.

In a pan over medium heat, gently sauté the onion and garlic in the butter until tender and translucent, about 5 minutes.

When the potatoes are cool enough to handle, cut them lengthwise. Let them cool a few minutes until you can handle them. Trying not to break the skins, scoop out the pulp, leaving about 1/4 inch | 5 mm on the skin. Discard or eat the skin that's in the worst shape. (Only 5 potatoes will fit on the average cooking plank, so the 6th potato half will just add volume to the filling.)

In a bowl, combine the pulp, sautéed vegetables, butter, cream, nutmeg and reserved 1 tsp | 5 mL of salt. Mash until smooth. Add the cheddar or Gouda and mix with a wooden spoon until the cheese is barely combined with the mash. Add extra milk or cream if the mix seems too dry. Spoon the filling into the potatoes, top with grated Parmesan and gently shape them with your hands if they've drooped a bit. Drizzle each potato with a little olive oil and sprinkle on a pinch of paprika.

Preheat the grill on medium-high for 5 or 10 minutes or until the chamber temperature rises above 500°F | 260°C. Rinse the plank and place it on the cooking grate. Cover the grill and heat the plank for 4 or 5 minutes, or until it starts to throw off a bit of smoke and crackles lightly. Reduce the heat to medium-low. Arrange the potatoes on the plank and cook for 10 to 15 minutes or until the cheese is nicely browned and blistered. Serve with sour cream and chopped chives.

PLANKED POLENTA ON THE BOARD
with grill-roasted mushrooms and goat cheese

Serves 4 to 6

Ted Reader kindly shared this planked classic with me. It first appeared in his great book, *On Fire in the Kitchen*. Ted is an incredible cook, and many of his dishes are over the top. If there's a lily, he's going to gild it. This recipe is no exception, and I wouldn't recommend it for novice cooks. For one thing, you need an extra-wide plank, which you'll have to get at a lumberyard or home improvement center. But, for those who take up the challenge, the result is an unusual feast on a plank that's sure to blow your guests away.

1 extra-wide untreated cedar plank (at least 8 inches | 20 cm wide by 12 inches | 30 cm long and 1/2 inch | 1 cm thick), soaked in cold water overnight or for at least 1 hour

1 large portobello mushroom cap

6 large white mushrooms

3 large oyster mushrooms

3 large shiitake mushroom caps

2 cups | 500 mL hot water

1/4 cup | 50 mL balsamic vinegar

1/4 cup | 50 mL olive oil

1 Tbsp | 15 mL Championship Barbecue Rub (page 29) or your favorite grilling rub

1 large sweet onion, cut into 1/2-inch | 1-cm rings

1 cup | 250 mL crumbled goat cheese

1 Tbsp | 15 mL chopped fresh basil

kosher salt and freshly ground black pepper

balsamic vinegar and olive oil

2 cups | 500 mL chicken stock

1 tsp | 5 mL salt

1 cup | 250 mL cornmeal

2 Tbsp | 25 mL butter

1/2 cup | 125 mL grated Asiago cheese

Preheat the grill to medium-high.

Place the cleaned mushrooms in a large bowl and add the hot water. Place a plate on top of the mushrooms to help keep them submerged. Let the mushrooms soak for 15 minutes. (This will keep them from drying out on the grill.) Drain the mushrooms and return to the bowl. In a separate bowl, mix together the vinegar, oil and barbecue rub. Pour over the mushrooms and toss to coat.

Grill the mushrooms (reserving the vinegar mixture), turning once, for 8 to 12 minutes or until tender and lightly charred.

Meanwhile, brush the onion rings with the reserved vinegar mixture and grill for 8 to 10 minutes, turning once, until lightly charred and tender.

Let the mushrooms and onions cool slightly, then cut into 1-inch | 2.5-cm chunks. In a bowl combine the mushrooms, onion rings, goat cheese and basil. Season to taste with salt, pepper and a dash or two of balsamic vinegar and olive oil. Set aside.

In a large saucepan, bring the chicken stock to a boil over high heat. Add 1 tsp | 5 mL salt. Reduce the heat to medium-low and add the cornmeal in a steady stream while whisking constantly. Then, using a wooden spoon, stir constantly for 15 to 20 minutes, until the cornmeal is thick and smooth. Remove from the heat.

Add the butter and 1/4 cup | 50 mL of the Asiago cheese, stirring until smooth. Season with salt and pepper. Let cool in the pot about 5 minutes.

Preheat the grill to high. Spoon the cooling polenta onto the cedar plank, piling it high and leaving a 1-inch | 2.5-cm border around the edge of the plank. Make a well in the center of the polenta and fill with the mushroom mixture. Sprinkle with the remaining Asiago cheese.

Place the plank on the center of the grill and close the lid. Bake for 10 to 15 minutes or until the polenta is lightly browned and hot. (If the plank ignites, reduce the heat and douse the flames using a spray bottle of water.)

Set the plank on a heatproof platter. Place in the center of the table and let your guests serve themselves.

PLANKED eggplant WITH FETA

Serves 4

My friend Stuart Parker shared this simple and delicious vegetarian recipe, which was designed for the grill, but works great on the plank.

1/3 cup | 75 mL extra virgin olive oil

2 Tbsp | 25 mL balsamic vinegar

2 cloves garlic, smashed or pushed through a press

1 medium European eggplant, cut into 3/4-inch | 2-cm rounds

1/2 cup | 125 mL crumbled feta cheese

Combine the olive oil, vinegar and garlic in a nonreactive pan that will hold the eggplant slices in one layer. Spoon half the marinade evenly over the slices, turn and spoon over the other half. Marinate for 30 to 60 minutes.

Preheat the grill on medium-high for 5 or 10 minutes or until the chamber temperature rises above 500°F | 260°C. Rinse the plank and place it on the cooking grate. Cover the grill and heat the plank for 4 or 5 minutes, or until it starts to throw off a bit of smoke and crackles lightly. Reduce the heat to medium and place the eggplant slices on the plank. Cover and cook for 10 minutes. Turn the slices over and top with the crumbled feta.

Continue cooking for about another 10 minutes, until the eggplant is cooked through and the cheese is nicely browned. Serve drizzled with a few drops of balsamic and a little more olive oil.

maple-planked BUTTERNUT squash purée

Serves 8 to 10

This squash dish, based on a recipe in Diane Rossen Worthington's great cookbook, *American Bistro*, goes with just about any meat. It can even be made early in the day if you've got an ambitious dinner on the go, like Thanksgiving. Reheat it gently in the microwave. I recommend organic carrots because they usually have so much flavor.

2 maple or alder cooking planks, soaked overnight or for at least 1 hour

2 butternut squashes, about 3 lb | 1.5 kg of flesh in total, peeled, seeded and cut into 1-inch | 2.5-cm slices

6 carrots, peeled

1 tsp | 5 mL ground ginger, or to taste

1 tsp | 5 mL maple syrup

3 Tbsp | 45 mL butter

2 Tbsp | 25 mL olive oil

kosher salt and freshly ground black pepper

1 Tbsp | 15 mL finely chopped parsley for garnish

Preheat the grill on medium-high for 5 or 10 minutes or until the chamber temperature rises above 500°F | 260°C. Rinse the planks and place them on the cooking grate, leaving at least 1 inch | 2.5 cm between them. Cover the grill and heat the planks for 4 or 5 minutes, or until they start to throw off a bit of smoke and crackle lightly. Reduce the heat to medium-low. Toss the squash slices and carrots with a little oil and distribute them evenly on the planks. Cover the grill and cook for 20 minutes, turning at the halfway mark. Test the vegetables for doneness by piercing them with a knife. When they're cooked through and nice and tender, transfer them to a plate or bowl to cool. The smaller pieces will be done earlier, so take them off first.

In a food processor, using the metal blade, combine the planked vegetables with all the ingredients except the parsley. Process until the mixture is smoothly puréed, scraping down the sides of the bowl as required and adding a little hot water if necessary. Taste for seasoning. Sprinkle with parsley and serve hot.

plank-roasted TOMATOES

Makes about 2 cups | 500 mL

This recipe lifts the flavor of the tomato to a higher plane with the use of salt, oil, rosemary and balsamic reduction. These are great warm as a side dish, but you can also cool them and incorporate them into a salad or chop them up and serve them on toasted baguette slices. In this case I recommend that you soak the plank for no more than an hour, which prevents warping, so your tomatoes are less likely to roll off.

1 maple, hickory, oak or mesquite plank, soaked no more than 1 hour

6 to 8 ripe tomatoes

kosher salt

sugar

1 Tbsp | 15 mL coarsely chopped fresh rosemary needles or 1 tsp | 5 mL dried rosemary

3 cloves garlic, finely chopped (optional)

2 Tbsp | 25 mL balsamic reduction (see page 46) or plain balsamic vinegar

1/4 cup | 50 mL extra virgin olive oil

Halve the tomatoes and place them, cut side up, on a cookie sheet. Season generously with salt and sugar, then sprinkle on the rosemary (and chopped garlic if you like). Drizzle with the balsamic and then the oil.

Preheat the grill on medium-high for 5 or 10 minutes or until the chamber temperature rises above 500°F | 260°C. Rinse the plank and place it on the cooking grate. Cover the grill and heat the plank for 4 or 5 minutes, or until it starts to throw off a bit of smoke and crackles lightly. Reduce the heat to low. Place the tomatoes cut-side up on the plank. (Alternatively, you can leave the tomatoes on the cookie sheet and place it on the plank.) Close the grill and cook on low for up to 2 hours, or until the tomatoes darken and shrivel.

THE GREAT UNPLANKED:
SIMPLE, TASTY STARTERS AND SIDES

Appetizers and side dishes should be easy to prepare, simple to present and delicious to eat. I like to focus my fussing energy on the meat! The following recipes are pure comfort foods, some of them quite humble, some a bit retro, all mmm-mmm good.

TOMATOES in paradise

Serves 4

Sometimes simple really is sensational.

3 Tbsp | 45 mL extra virgin olive oil

1 Tbsp | 15 mL lemon juice

1 tsp | 5 mL Dijon mustard

1 clove finely chopped or pressed garlic

1 Tbsp | 15 mL chopped fresh herbs (mint, basil, rosemary, etc.)

kosher salt and freshly ground black pepper

4 exceptional tomatoes, cut into quarters

1/2 cup | 125 mL chopped red onion

1 cup | 250 mL kalamata or other Mediterranean olives

In a salad bowl, whisk together the olive oil, lemon juice, mustard, garlic and herbs. Season with salt and pepper. Toss with the other ingredients. Let stand for half an hour at room temperature, then serve.

GARDEN salsa

Makes about 1 cup | 250 mL

I love the crunch of barely cooked asparagus. Why don't we ever eat it raw? This salsa showcases the texture and flavor of fresh asparagus, which is a bit like snap peas, in a spectacularly colorful combination. This is excellent with any kind of seafood.

4 spears extremely fresh asparagus, tough ends
discarded and spears diced

1/4 cup | 50 mL diced yellow bell pepper

1/4 cup | 50 mL diced purple onion

1 medium-sized ripe tomato, diced

1 tsp | 5 mL chopped fresh dill

juice of 1/2 lemon

1 tsp | 5 mL sugar

pinch cayenne pepper

kosher salt

Combine all the ingredients in a salad bowl, toss and serve.

BEET this!

Serves 6 to 8

In late summer, when these vegetables are all at their finest, this salad may be unbeatable. You'll have to plan ahead for it so the beets are ready when you need them. Macedonian feta is smoothly tart, but other fetas will do.

10 beets, medium-sized, in several colours, if possible

1 lemon, juice and zest (grated or finely minced)

1 orange, juice and zest (grated or finely minced)

1 Tbsp | 15 mL sherry vinegar

1 Tbsp | 15 mL chopped fresh tarragon

1 Tbsp | 15 mL chopped fresh chives

kosher salt and freshly ground black pepper

6 cups | 1.5 L mesclun mix (mixed greens)

1/2 to 3/4 cup | 125 to 175 mL feta cheese (preferably Macedonian), crumbled

18 cherry tomatoes, in different colors, if possible

1/2 cup | 125 mL walnuts or pecans, toasted and chopped (optional)

Preheat the oven to 400°F (200°C). Trim the beets, leaving the skin on. Place them in a pan and roast for about 45 minutes, or until you can pierce them to the center with a knife. Remove and cool. When they're cool enough to handle, peel the beets and dice them into bite-sized pieces. In a small bowl, combine the lemon, orange, vinegar, tarragon and chives. Whisk together and season to taste with salt and pepper.

Toss the remaining ingredients with the beets and vinaigrette and serve immediately.

Kate's **CHUNKY** slaw

Serves 6

This rough and tumble slaw is easy to make and even easier to eat. The fresh, satisfyingly crunchy texture of the cabbage is complemented by the tangy apple chunks and the sweet, soft raisins. This isn't a juicy slaw; the mayo clings to the ingredients more like a dip than a dressing.

**1 medium head white cabbage,
cut into bite-sized chunks**

1 cup | 250 mL mayonnaise

**2 crisp, tangy apples, peeled and
cut into bite-sized chunks**

1/2 cup | 125 mL raisins

kosher salt and freshly ground black pepper

Toss the ingredients together and serve immediately.

classic LEXINGTON-STYLE slaw

Serves 8

This tangy, fiery slaw is great with strongly flavored meats. But I hear that in Lexington, North Carolina, they serve this with, and on, everything.

1 medium head white cabbage

3 Tbsp | 45 mL liquid honey

1 cup | 250 mL cider vinegar

2/3 cup | 150 mL ketchup

pinch cayenne pepper

pinch crushed dried red chiles

3/4 tsp | 4 mL kosher salt, or to taste

dash Louisana-style hot sauce

Grate or shred the cabbage. Combine the remaining ingredients in a saucepan and bring to a low boil. Simmer over medium heat for 10 minutes. Pour the warm sauce over the cabbage, toss and serve immediately.

ASIAN slaw

Serves 4 to 6

Asian-flavored meat demands an Asian-inspired slaw, and the peanuts add a nice crunch.

For the dressing:

2 Tbsp | 25 mL soy sauce

2 Tbsp | 25 mL rice vinegar

1 tsp | 5 mL toasted sesame oil

1^1/$_2$ tsp | 7 mL finely minced ginger

1 tsp | 5 mL Vietnamese chili sauce

1/4 cup | 50 mL creamy peanut butter

1 tsp | 5 mL sugar

1 or 2 tsp | 5 or 10 mL water (if needed)

For the salad:

2 cups | 500 mL savoy or napa cabbage,
grated or shredded into fine slices

1 cup | 250 mL purple cabbage,
grated or shredded into fine slices

1 carrot, peeled and grated

1 green onion, chopped

1 small red bell pepper, julienned

2 Tbsp | 25 mL fresh chopped cilantro

1/4 cup | 50 mL fresh bean sprouts

1/4 cup | 50 mL dry-roasted peanuts,
coarsely chopped, for garnish

Combine the dressing ingredients and whisk together, adding water a little at a time until the mixture is a smooth, fairly thick liquid. Toss with the vegetables and serve immediately, garnished with the chopped peanuts.

watermelon SALAD

Serves 4

Sometimes the simplest combinations work the best. This one, created by my friend Michelle Allaire, is as refreshing as it sounds.

1/2 watermelon, rind removed and flesh cut into 1-inch | 2.5-cm chunks

1/2 lb | 250 g feta cheese, cut into small chunks

juice of 1 lemon

3 Tbsp | 45 mL olive oil

freshly ground black pepper

Place the watermelon chunks in a salad bowl. Add the feta cheese. In a separate bowl, mix together the lemon juice, olive oil and a grinding of black pepper. Add the dressing at the last minute, just before serving.

PAULINE'S wild RICE salad

Serves 4 to 6

I had this salad at a wedding reception and just had to have the recipe, which Pauline Bahnsen kindly shared with me. She says it's quite versatile, and she has made substitutions and additions over the years (you can substitute dried cranberries for the raisins or use whatever kind of rice you want). It's a great party salad because it keeps well when made the day before. If you're cooking it for a wedding, you can also easily multiply the ingredients to suit the size of the crowd you're serving.

For the salad:

$2^{1}/_{4}$ cups | 550 mL water

1/4 tsp | 1 mL kosher salt

3/4 cup | 175 mL brown basmati rice or brown rice

1/2 cup | 125 mL wild rice (or substitute other kinds of rice to increase variety of textures and tastes)

one 8-oz | 227-mL can water chestnuts, drained and sliced

1 green bell pepper, diced

1 red bell pepper, diced

2 stalks celery, diced

1/2 cup | 125 mL raisins

1/2 cup | 125 mL diced red onion

1/2 cup | 125 mL chopped toasted almonds

1/4 cup | 50 mL chopped fresh parsley

For the dressing:

1/3 cup | 75 mL orange or grapefruit juice

1 Tbsp | 15 mL finely chopped or grated lemon zest

2 Tbsp | 30 mL lemon juice

2 Tbsp | 25 mL tamari or soy sauce

1 Tbsp | 15 mL vegetable oil

1 large clove garlic, minced

1 Tbsp | 15 mL dry sherry vinegar or rice vinegar

1/4 tsp | 1 mL kosher salt

In a small saucepan, bring $2^{1}/_{4}$ cups | 550 mL of water to a boil. Add the salt and rice; reduce the heat, cover and simmer until the rice is tender and no liquid remains, about 45 minutes, depending on the rice mixture used. Transfer to a large bowl. Add the water chestnuts, bell peppers, celery, raisins, onion, almonds and parsley, tossing to combine.

In a small bowl, whisk together the dressing ingredients. Pour over the salad and toss to coat. This can be made ahead and refrigerated for up to 24 hours.

EASY ALABAMA potato salad

Serves 8

I once met a lovely woman from Alabama on a plane, and I quizzed her on what she and her family liked to eat in the summertime. She shared this quick, pantry-based recipe for a potato salad that's bound to bring back memories of happy times for anyone. I've added a favorite ingredient, toasted pecans, to give it some extra crunch.

3 lb | 1.5 kg yellow-fleshed potatoes

1 cup | 250 mL mayonnaise

1 Tbsp | 15 mL green hot dog relish

1 Tbsp | 15 mL prepared mustard

1 tsp | 5 mL sugar

1 tsp | 5 mL white vinegar

1/2 red onion, cut into bite-sized pieces

sweet paprika and chopped chives or green onion for garnish

1/2 cup | 125 mL toasted pecans, coarsely chopped (optional)

Peel the potatoes and cut them into quarters. Place in a large pot of cold salted water. Over high heat bring the water to a boil. Reduce the heat and simmer for 10 to 15 minutes, until the potatoes are almost done. Drain and let the potatoes cool to room temperature.

Cut the potatoes into bite-sized pieces. In a large bowl combine the mayo, relish, mustard, sugar and vinegar. Toss the dressing with the red onion and potatoes. Transfer to a serving dish and garnish with a dusting of paprika, a sprinkling of chopped chives or green onion, and the chopped pecans if desired.

SALMON salad

This classic salad leaps to another level when made with salmon that is infused with smoke.

1 lb | 500 g leftover salmon, broken into flakes

1 stalk celery, chopped

1 Tbsp | 15 mL capers (the small kind)

6 pitted green olives, coarsely chopped

1 Tbsp | 15 mL chopped fresh mint

1 Tbsp | 15 mL chopped fresh parsley

1/2 cup | 125 mL mayonnaise

2 Tbsp | 25 mL honey mustard

juice of 1/2 lemon

1 dill pickle, coarsely chopped

kosher salt and freshly ground black pepper

1 head butter lettuce, separated into
individual leaves

lemon wedges and mint sprigs for garnish

Combine all the ingredients except the lettuce, lemon wedges and mint sprigs in a nonreactive bowl. Spoon the salad into the lettuce leaves and garnish with the mint and lemon.

kickin' CRAB salad

Serves 4 to 6

Read this recipe, invented by my friend Diane Read, and tell me if your mouth doesn't start watering. This tangy, spicy, colorful salad is just the thing to get your guests' appetites going, or as a main dish for a summer lunch. Serve with a crisp, dry, fruity white wine.

**1 lb | 500 g Dungeness or snow crab meat
(make sure there are a few whole claw pieces
in the mix to make it look pretty)**

**2 Tbsp | 25 mL each finely chopped red bell pepper,
green onion and long English cucumber**

1/2 small lemon

1/2 cup | 125 mL regular or light mayonnaise

2 tsp | 10 mL wasabi paste (or more to your taste)

1/4 tsp | 1 mL crushed dried red chiles

1 head butter lettuce, leaves separated

lemon wedges or slices for garnish

Place the crab in a large bowl. Carefully fold the red pepper, onion and cucumber into the crab and squeeze lemon juice over. Mix together the mayonnaise, wasabi paste and chiles, and fold into the crab mixture.

Wash and dry the butter lettuce and either line a platter with small leaves for appetizers or place large leaves on individual plates. Use an ice cream scoop or tablespoon to place the crab mixture on the lettuce leaves. Garnish with lemon.

wilted summer LETTUCE salad

Serves 4

This is my version of a wilted lettuce salad I grew up on. The slight bitterness of the lettuce, the sweet and sour creaminess of the dressing and the crunch of the vegetables are a combination that will bring the sun out on your palate even if it's pouring rain outside.

For the dressing:

1/2 cup | 125 mL mayonnaise

1/2 cup | 125 mL white vinegar

2 Tbsp | 25 mL sugar

1/4 cup | 50 mL whipping cream

For the salad:

1 head leaf lettuce, preferably right from your garden, washed and torn into bite-sized pieces

1 green onion, chopped

4 radishes, thinly sliced

1/2 cup | 125 mL sliced cucumber

1 Tbsp | 15 mL chopped fresh dill
(or 1 tsp | 10 mL dried dill)

freshly ground black pepper

Whisk together the dressing ingredients and heat in a saucepan, stirring, until the mixture is hot but not boiling. Toss the vegetables together and place them in a sealable plastic container. Pour the hot dressing over the salad, add the dill, toss, and seal the container. Let sit for half an hour, toss again and serve with a grinding of black pepper.

grilled ASPARAGUS

Serves 4 as a side dish

This is one dish that wouldn't benefit from plank-cooking. The key here is to grill the asparagus very quickly over high heat, so it chars on the outside but remains almost raw in the center. The flavor and texture of this easy dish can earn you more wows than far more complicated recipes. And it's good for you, too.

1 bunch (about 20 spears) fresh asparagus
(choose very fresh asparagus that's relatively thick;
pencil-thin spears don't stand up to grilling well)

extra virgin olive oil

kosher salt

1/2 lemon

Wash and trim the asparagus and pat dry in a paper towel. Transfer to a large bowl or dish. Preheat your grill on high until the chamber temperature rises above 500°F | 260°C. Drizzle olive oil on the asparagus and sprinkle with kosher salt. With your hands, toss to coat the spears evenly with the oil and salt.

Place the asparagus spears on the hot grill, taking care to put them across the cooking grate so they won't fall through. Close the grill and cook for just 1 or 2 minutes. Turn the spears with a set of tongs, close the grill and cook for another minute or two. The asparagus will turn an intense green and will have nice little char marks. Transfer the spears back to the bowl and immediately squeeze the lemon over them, tossing to coat. Serve immediately as an appetizer or side dish, or cool and add to a vegetable platter. Grilled asparagus goes extremely well with doctored mayos (see pages 45–46).

rosemary ROASTED CARROTS

Serves 6

Carrots on the grill? Yes indeed. Plain old carrots take on magical characteristics when roasted slowly on a grill. Serve them with pork, lamb or beef, or as part of an appetizer platter with some doctored mayo (see pages 45–46).

12 carrots

extra virgin olive oil

kosher salt

dried rosemary needles

Trim the tops and bottoms of the carrots. Scrub well but leave the skin on. Drizzle with olive oil and sprinkle on some salt and crushed rosemary needles. Toss to coat the carrots and put them on a medium grill over direct heat for half an hour to an hour, or until they're nicely charred and cooked through. Drizzle a little more olive oil on them just before serving.

Florida GRILLED zucchini

Serves 4

Why Florida? In 1990 there was a feature in *Gourmet* magazine about dinner in Florida. Must have been about low-cal eating for the diet-conscious retiree. That's all I remember, except for this incredibly simple and delicious grilled zucchini. I made it to accompany roast turkey on Thanksgiving that year. My wife had toiled for days on the dinner and had cooked an elaborate and complicated turkey recipe. When the meal was served, it was the zucchini that got the raves, not me. Right, honey? By the way, this is one of the few grilled dishes, along with grilled asparagus, that I wouldn't cook on a plank. Why mess with a good thing?

1 large clove garlic, minced and mashed to a paste with 1/2 tsp | 2 mL kosher salt

2 Tbsp | 25 mL fresh lemon juice

1 tsp | 5 mL white wine vinegar

1/4 cup | 150 mL vegetable oil

freshly ground black pepper

2 zucchini (each about 1½ inches | 4 cm in diameter), scrubbed

Whisk together the garlic paste, lemon juice, vinegar, oil and pepper. Pour the mixture into a large baking dish. Halve the zucchini lengthwise and toss the pieces in the marinade, making sure they're well-coated. Cover and refrigerate overnight, turning the zucchini several times.

Prepare your grill for medium heat. Grill the zucchini for 4 or 5 minutes, cut side down. Turn them, brush with some marinade, and grill the other side for 4 or 5 more minutes or until they're just tender. Transfer to a cutting board, slice them diagonally and serve. This is a perfect dish to make while a large cut of meat is off the grill and resting.

fettucini ALFREDO

Serves 4

This classic pasta is a great accompaniment to any planked food.

1 Tbsp | 15 mL kosher salt

1 cup | 250 mL heavy cream

1/4 cup | 50 mL butter

1 lb | 500 g fettuccini

1/2 cup | 125 mL grated Parmesan cheese

1/4 tsp | 1 mL freshly grated nutmeg or to taste

kosher salt and freshly ground black pepper

Fill a large pot with water, add salt and bring to a rolling boil. Add the pasta to the boiling water and cook until it is *al dente*. Meanwhile, pour the cream into a saucepan over medium heat. Add the butter and stir until the mixture starts to simmer. Just before the pasta is ready to drain, add the cheese to the cream and butter mixture and stir to incorporate. Add the grated nutmeg and season with salt and pepper (don't forget, the cheese is already quite salty). Drain the pasta and toss with the sauce. Serve immediately with extra Parmesan on the side.

ALLAN'S CHILE **corn** cakes

Serves 6

These slightly spicy corn cakes, or fritters, are a specialty of my brother Allan, a fabulous cook. They're fantastic with grilled or planked meats and fish, especially salmon.

1/4 cup | 50 mL olive oil

1 cup | 250 mL chopped red bell pepper

1/4 cup | 50 mL chopped yellow bell pepper

2 cups | 500 mL fresh raw corn kernels
(about 4 large ears)

2/3 cup | 150 mL chopped yellow onion

1 Tbsp | 15 mL pure chili powder

1 tsp | 5 mL ground cumin

1/4 cup | 50 mL rich chicken stock

3/4 cup | 175 mL all-purpose flour

1 tsp | 5 mL baking powder

1/2 cup | 125 mL yellow cornmeal

1 egg, lightly beaten

1/2 cup | 125 mL milk

1 Tbsp | 15 mL melted unsalted butter

2 Tbsp | 25 mL chopped cilantro

kosher salt and freshly ground black pepper

more vegetable oil for sautéing

sour cream, cilantro and chopped jalapeños for garnish

Heat 2 Tbsp | 25 mL of the olive oil in a large saucepan over medium-high heat and sauté the peppers, corn and onion for 2 to 3 minutes. Add the chili powder and cumin and cook for 2 minutes, stirring constantly. Add the chicken stock and stir, scraping up any brown bits from the bottom of the pan. Continue cooking until most of the liquid has evaporated. Set aside.

Sift the flour and baking powder into a small bowl. Add the cornmeal, egg, milk and butter and stir until very smooth. Add the corn mixture and cilantro and season with salt and pepper.

Heat the remaining 2 Tbsp | 25 mL of vegetable oil in a large sauté pan over medium-high heat. Add the corn batter in large dollops and sauté until golden brown, about 3 to 4 minutes per side. Remove to paper towels and drain. Cook in batches and add oil if necessary.

Serve garnished with sour cream, cilantro and chopped jalapeños, if desired. "Eat these hot and try not to steal them from the pan," says Allan. "Good luck once you've tasted one!"

roasted GARLIC MASHED potatoes

Serves 4 to 6

If you're calorie-conscious you can substitute milk or chicken stock for the cream in this recipe, but the point of this dish is to celebrate decadence, so I suggest adding extra butter, cream and truffle oil to taste. This dish goes well with almost any planked meat or fish.

2 lb | 1 kg yellow-fleshed potatoes

1 head roasted garlic (see sidebar page 43)

1/2 cup | 125 mL butter, at room temperature

1/2 cup | 125 mL heavy cream

1/4 tsp | 1 mL freshly grated nutmeg

1 Tbsp | 15 mL finely chopped parsley

1 tsp | 15 mL truffle oil (optional)

kosher salt and freshly ground black pepper

Peel the potatoes and cut them into quarters. Place in a large pot and fill with cold water to cover. Over high heat bring to a boil and then reduce to medium for 15 to 20 minutes, or until a fork goes easily through a chunk of potato. Drain and return to the pot, reserving a cup or so of the water. Add the roasted garlic, butter, cream, nutmeg, parsley and truffle oil, if desired, and mash until creamy. If the mixture seems too dry, moisten with a little potato water. Season with salt and pepper. Inhale.

wasabi MASHED potatoes

Serves 6 to 8

You don't always have to serve rice with Asian dishes. This mashed potato recipe is easy to make and packs an unexpected punch. You can get wasabi paste in Asian specialty stores.

3 lb | 1.5 kg yellow-fleshed potatoes

**3/4 cup | 175 mL cream (or whole milk if you
are worried about your fat intake)**

1 Tbsp | 15 mL wasabi paste

1/4 cup | 50 mL butter at room temperature

kosher salt and freshly ground black pepper

Peel the potatoes and place them in a large pot of cold water. Bring to a boil and cook until tender, about 20 minutes. Drain the potatoes, reserving 1/2 cup | 125 mL of the liquid. Mash until smooth. Combine the cream or milk and wasabi in a small bowl and mix until smooth. Add the wasabi mixture to the potatoes and mash thoroughly, adding some reserved potato liquid if necessary, until creamy smooth. Season with salt and pepper and serve hot.

cuban-STYLE BLACK beans

Serves 6 to 8

This dish, along with some white rice, is a great accompaniment to planked meats, particularly those with Southwestern and barbecue flavors. It also goes great with ham and eggs.

1/4 cup | 50 mL olive oil

1 medium onion, chopped

1 green bell pepper, seeded and chopped

6 cloves garlic, chopped

1 Tbsp | 15 mL dried oregano

1 tsp | 15 mL ground cumin

two 19-oz | 540-mL cans black beans, rinsed and drained

3/4 cup | 175 mL chicken stock or water

1½ Tbsp | 20 mL cider vinegar

1 tsp | 5 mL sugar

kosher salt and freshly ground black pepper

Heat the oil in a heavy pot over medium heat. Add the onion, bell pepper, garlic, oregano and cumin, and sauté until the vegetables start to soften, about 5 minutes.

Add about a cup | 250 mL of the beans and mash them with the back of a fork. Add the rest of the beans, the stock or water and the vinegar. Simmer, stirring often, for about 15 minutes or until the mixture thickens. Stir in the sugar. Season with salt and pepper and serve.

lime-GINGER risotto

Serves 4

This recipe was invented by sophisticated teenager Carolyn Rowan, whose family was faced one day with a nearly empty fridge. Carolyn improvised the recipe, using ingredients at hand, and created a classic. This risotto is great as a first course or as a side with seafood.

2 Tbsp | 25 mL olive oil

1 white onion, chopped

3 cloves garlic, finely chopped

2 cups | 500 mL arborio rice

4 cups | 1 L chicken stock

1 cup | 250 mL dry white wine

zest of 1/2 lime, finely minced or grated

juice of 1 lime

1/2 cup | 125 mL grated Parmesan cheese

2 Tbsp | 25 mL whipping cream

kosher salt and freshly ground black pepper

Heat the oil in a saucepan or deep frying pan over medium heat. When the oil is hot, add the chopped onion and garlic. Sauté for 2 minutes, taking care not to burn the vegetables. Add the rice. Stir until the rice is opaque, about 5 minutes. Add 1 cup of the chicken stock and stir until the liquid is absorbed. Continue to add the chicken stock, 1 cup at a time, stirring constantly and adding more liquid when the last cup has been absorbed. Stir in the wine, lime zest, lime juice and Parmesan. The dish is done when the rice is *al dente* and the mixture is creamy, like a thick porridge. Just before serving, add the whipping cream. Season with salt and pepper and serve immediately.

salmon CAKES

Serves 8 as an appetizer or 4 as a main course

Fish cakes make a great appetizer or a light meal, and if you make good use of this book you're going to have some leftover salmon from time to time. Make smaller cakes for finger-food appetizers and larger ones for meal-sized portions.

**2 cups | 500 mL leftover planked salmon
(or any other cooked firm-fleshed fish)**

3 cups | 750 mL cold Roasted Garlic Mashed Potatoes (page 96)

2 Tbsp | 25 mL butter

1 medium onion, finely chopped

1 tsp | 5 mL curry powder (optional)

pinch cayenne pepper

2 Tbsp | 25 mL chopped cilantro or flat-leaf Italian parsley

kosher salt and freshly ground black pepper

1 egg, well beaten

1 cup | 250 mL panko (Japanese bread crumbs)

1/4 cup | 50 mL canola oil or other neutral-flavored cooking oil

Curry Mayo (optional; recipe page 46)

cilantro or parsley sprigs for garnish

Break the salmon into flakes with your hands. Put the flaked salmon and mashed potatoes in a mixing bowl and set aside. Heat the butter in a skillet over medium heat. When it just starts to foam, add the onion. Cook for 2 or 3 minutes until the onion is translucent. Add the curry powder and cook, stirring, for 1 more minute. Transfer the onions into the bowl with the potatoes, add the cayenne pepper and chopped cilantro or parsley and mix thoroughly with your hands, taking care not to make the mixture too mushy. Taste the mixture and season with salt and pepper to taste.

Shape the mixture into cakes about 3/4 inch | 2 cm thick. Dip the cakes in the egg and roll them gently in the bread crumbs.

Wipe any stray bits of onion from the skillet and put it on medium heat. Add the oil. When the oil starts to shimmer, add the fish cakes, making sure not to overcrowd them in the pan. Cook for 3 to 5 minutes, until the bottoms are golden brown and crispy, and carefully turn them, cooking on the other side for another 3 to 5 minutes. These are delicate, so handle them gently!

Transfer the finished cakes to a platter. To serve, place a dollop of Curry Mayo on top of each cake and garnish with cilantro or parsley sprigs.

SEAFOOD

Chapter 4

Whoever invented modern planking probably cooked a side of salmon on a cedar plank. But when it comes to plank-cooking seafood, there's so much more to explore. Seafood is perfectly suited to this style of grilling, which protects the delicate flesh of the fish from overcooking and adds an interesting flavor. These recipes will broaden your mind and put some salt spray on your palate.

CLASSIC PLANKED SALMON RECIPES

Salmon is by far the most popular dish cooked on a plank, so I'm dedicating a whole section of this book to plank-cooking this majestic and delicious fish.

cedar-planked **salmon** with WHISKEY-MAPLE GLAZE

Serves 6 to 8

In a way, this recipe spawned the book you're holding. I've cooked it scores of times over the past couple of years and I often get the comment, "This is the best salmon I've ever eaten." The sweet, woody flavor of the Jack Daniel's and maple syrup complements the richness of the salmon and the aroma of the cedar in this West Coast dish. I like to present it on the plank and then serve it on a bed of field greens tossed with some French walnut oil, kosher salt and toasted pumpkin seeds.

NOTE: The original recipe called for cooking on high heat, for about 5 minutes less time. With practice I've learned that it's better to get the plank smoking at high heat, but to turn down the grill and cook the salmon a little longer at a lower temperature. This allows it to cook more gently and evenly.

1 cedar cooking plank, soaked overnight or at least 1 hour

1/2 cup | 125 mL Jack Daniel's Tennessee Whiskey

1 cup | 250 mL real maple syrup

1 tsp | 5 mL crushed hot red chiles

1 Tbsp | 15 mL butter at room temperature

1 whole, boned fillet wild Pacific salmon
(about 3 lb | 1.5 kg), skin on

kosher salt and freshly ground black pepper

1 tsp | 5 mL granulated onion (or onion powder
if you can't find granules)

2 lemons, halved

parsley sprigs for garnish

1 Tbsp | 15 mL finely chopped flat-leaf Italian parsley

continues on next page ...

TYPES OF
⪢ SALMON ⪡

For North American consumers there are basically five kinds of salmon available on the market.

Chinook: Also known as spring or king salmon, this is my favorite fish, with firm flesh, good fat content and exceptional flavor. The most exotic and delicious of all salmon is the white spring or white king, which has a light pink, almost ivory-colored flesh. I think it's best for plank-cooking because it's the largest of the salmon species, which means you can often get 4 or 5 lb | 1.8 to 2.2 kg fillets, or even larger. At its freshest, spring salmon has flesh so firm and flavorful it reminds me of lobster meat.

Sockeye: Sockeye has a bright red-orange color and rich, tasty flesh. It is a smaller breed, with fillets in the 2 to 3 lb (1 to 1.5 kg) range. It's tasty but easy to overcook on the plank because of its small size.

Coho: This is the feistiest of west coast game fish, renowned for its habit of leaping out of the water while being reeled in. If you can get wild coho, buy it and try it. It's really succulent, and sometimes you can get fairly big fillets.

Chum: Leaner and lighter in color than its cousins, the chum is delicious but milder in flavor than the bigger species.

Pink: I love fresh pink salmon, although it's not as good for plank-cooking because it's the smallest and leanest of the salmon species. But it has a lovely delicate flavor and light-colored flesh that make it excellent for pan-frying or quick-roasting.

Make the sauce by combining the whiskey and maple syrup. In a small saucepan, bring the mixture to a low boil and reduce by about half, until you have a thick syrup that coats the back of a spoon. Add the chiles and butter and stir until just combined. Set aside and keep warm on the stovetop.

Season the skinless side of the salmon with salt, pepper and granulated onion. Let the salmon sit for 10 or 15 minutes at room temperature, until the rub is moistened.

While the salmon is sitting, preheat the grill on medium-high for 5 or 10 minutes or until the chamber temperature rises above 500°F | 260°C. Rinse the plank and place it on the cooking grate. Cover the grill and heat the plank for 4 or 5 minutes, or until it starts to throw off a bit of smoke and crackles lightly. Reduce the heat to medium-low. Season the plank with kosher salt and place the salmon, skin side down, on the plank.

Cover the grill and cook for 15 to 20 minutes or until the fish has an internal temperature of 135°F | 57°C. Check periodically to make sure the plank doesn't catch fire, and spray the burning edges with water if it does, making sure to close the lid afterwards.

When the salmon is done, squeeze half a lemon along its length and carefully transfer to a platter. Garnish with parsley sprigs and the remaining lemon cut into slices. Bring the salmon to the table. Drizzle a spoonful of the sauce over each portion as you serve and sprinkle with a little chopped parsley.

the FIRE chef's BBQ salmon on a plank

Serves 4 to 6

The late David Veljacic was the father of barbecue in Canada, founding the Canadian National Barbecue Championship in New Westminster. David was a firefighter, hence his nickname The Fire Chef. He was diagnosed with cancer several years before he succumbed to it in 2001, and while on medical leave he wrote cookbooks and taught barbecue and grilling to a generation of backyard cooks. This is his most famous recipe, adapted for the plank.

For the marinade:

1/3 cup | 75 mL finely chopped parsley

3 Tbsp | 45 mL oil-packed sun-dried tomatoes, finely chopped

1 Tbsp | 15 mL oil from the sun-dried tomatoes

1/3 cup | 75 mL extra virgin olive oil

For the salmon:

1 alder or hickory plank, soaked overnight or at least 1 hour

one 2½-lb | 1.2-kg boned salmon fillet, skin on

1 tsp | 5 mL kosher salt

1 head roasted garlic (see sidebar page 43), cloves squeezed out of their skins

Combine the marinade ingredients. Place the fillet in a nonreactive dish (a lasagna pan would do). Pour the marinade over the fillet. Cover with plastic wrap and refrigerate overnight.

Score the salmon with 2 long slits along the length of the fillet. Don't cut all the way through the fish. Mash the salt together with the roasted garlic and spread the mixture over the fillet and into the slits. Re-coat the fillet with the marinade after you've spread the garlic paste over it.

Preheat the grill on medium-high for 5 or 10 minutes or until the chamber temperature rises above 500°F | 260°C. Rinse the plank and place it on the cooking grate. Cover the grill and heat the plank for 4 or 5 minutes, or until it starts to throw off a bit of smoke and crackles lightly. Place the salmon on the plank and reduce the heat to medium-low. Cook for 15 to 20 minutes or until the fish has an internal temperature of 135°F | 57°C. Remove the plank and the salmon from the grill and serve.

THE K.C. BARON'S
hickory-planked salmon
WITH BROWN SUGAR CURE

Serves 8 to 10

What can I say about Paul Kirk? He's the one and only Kansas City Baron of Barbecue, a seven-time world champion and a true barbecue pioneer. He has been generous enough to adapt one of his favorite salmon recipes for the plank especially for this book. If you're ever in New York City, don't forget to visit his new restaurant, R.U.B. (Righteous Urban Barbecue).

1 large hickory plank, soaked overnight or at least 1 hour in water or apple juice

2 cups | 500 mL dark brown sugar

1 Tbsp | 15 mL Morton Tender Quick (a cure mixture available in the spice or salt section in grocery stores)

1 Tbsp | 15 mL Old Bay Seasoning or Seafood Seasoning Blend (recipe follows)

2 tsp | 10 mL coarsely ground black pepper

2 tsp | 10 mL kosher salt

1 tsp | 5 mL granulated garlic

one 5-lb | 2.2-kg fillet of salmon, pin bones removed

1/2 cup | 125 mL Dijon mustard

Combine 1 cup | 250 mL of the brown sugar with the Tender Quick, Old Bay, pepper, salt and garlic and blend well.

Place the salmon on a large piece of plastic wrap. Sprinkle the skin side of the fillet with the sugar mixture, turn over and cover the fillet with the rest of the sugar mixture. Wrap the fillet up in the plastic wrap, place in the refrigerator and let marinate or cure for 2 hours.

When you're ready to cook the salmon, remove it from the refrigerator. Using a pastry brush, paint the top side of the salmon fillet with the mustard and coat with the remaining 1 cup | 250 mL of brown sugar.

Preheat the grill on medium-high for 5 or 10 minutes or until the chamber temperature rises above 500°F | 260°C. Rinse the plank and place it on the cooking grate. Cover the grill and heat the plank for 4 or 5 minutes, or until it starts to throw off a bit of smoke and crackles lightly. Reduce the heat to medium-low.

Place the salmon on the plank and cook for 20 to 25 minutes or until the fish has an internal temperature of 135°F | 57°C.

NOTE: The standard instructions in this book are for planking with a gas grill. Paul is a died-in-the-wool charcoal-and-hardwood guy, and his recipe calls for this dish to be cooked in a covered charcoal grill. He recommends a 35- to 40-minute cooking time, with some hickory chips thrown onto the coals for good measure.

Seafood Seasoning Blend

Makes 1/4 cup | 50 mL

You can use this as a substitute for Old Bay or other seafood seasonings. It's good on chicken as well.

1 Tbsp | 15 mL ground bay leaves

2$\frac{1}{2}$ tsp | 12 mL celery salt

1$\frac{1}{2}$ tsp | 7 mL dry mustard

1$\frac{1}{2}$ tsp | 7 mL ground black pepper

3/4 tsp | 3 mL ground nutmeg

1/2 tsp | 2 mL ground cloves

1/2 tsp | 2 mL ground ginger

1/2 tsp | 2 mL paprika

1/2 tsp | 2 mL cayenne pepper

Combine well and store in an airtight container.

PLANKING ⤐ SECRET ⤏

Plank-cooking works well in both gas and charcoal grills. As long as it's a covered grill, you'll get the desired smoky flavor from the smoldering plank. If you do use a charcoal grill to do your planking, add a few minutes to the cooking time. Covered charcoal grills generally produce a more moderate heat compared to natural gas and propane grills.

STEVEN RAICHLEN'S PLANKED salmon with mustard and dill sauce

Serves 4

Steven Raichlen is Zeus in the pantheon of barbecue cooking gods, and I'm honored to include this recipe from his book *BBQ USA*. His technique is a little different from mine, but it works just as well.

1 cedar plank, soaked overnight or at least 1 hour

1 boned salmon fillet, with or without skin (about 1½ lb | 750 g; ideally cut from the end closest to the head)

olive oil for brushing

coarse salt (kosher or sea) and freshly ground black pepper

1/2 cup | 125 mL mayonnaise (preferably Hellmann's)

1/3 cup | 75 mL grainy French mustard

2 Tbsp | 25 mL chopped fresh dill

1/2 tsp | 2 mL finely grated lemon zest

If using salmon with skin, generously brush the skin with olive oil. If using skinless salmon, brush one side of the fish with olive oil. Season both sides with salt and pepper. Place the salmon on the plank, skin side down if it has one, oiled side down if not.

Place the mayonnaise, mustard, dill and lemon zest in a nonreactive mixing bowl and whisk to mix. Season with salt and pepper to taste.

Set up the grill for indirect grilling and preheat to medium-high. (Indirect grilling means placing whatever you're cooking on a part of the cooking grate that isn't directly above hot coals or a gas flame.) When ready to cook, spread the glaze mixture evenly over the top and sides of the salmon. Place the salmon on its plank in the center of the hot grate, away from the heat, and cover the grill. Cook the salmon until cooked through and the glaze is a deep golden brown, 20 to 30 minutes. To test for doneness, insert an instant-read meat thermometer through the side of the salmon: the internal temperature should be about 135°F | 57°C. Another test is to insert a slender metal skewer in the side of the fillet for 20 seconds: It should come out very hot to the touch. Transfer the plank and fish to a heatproof platter and slice the fish crosswise into serving portions. Serve the salmon right off the plank.

NOTE: You can use fish fillets with or without skin—your choice. (Though Steven loves the skin, he says his wife finds that it makes the salmon taste fishy. He recommends this recipe for other rich, oily fish fillets, including bluefish and pompano.)

PLANKING ∼ SECRET ∼

Removing the skin from a salmon fillet is pretty easy if you have a sharp, flexible fillet knife. Just start an incision near the tail of the fillet. As you cut, hold the end of the skin down and keep downward pressure on the knife. The skin is tough enough so you won't cut through. If this is too daunting a task, ask your fishmonger to do it for you.

CHEF howie's PLANKEDsalmon

Serves 4

John Howie could be considered a planking pioneer. As executive chef of Seastar Restaurant & Raw Bar in Bellevue, Washington, and purveyor of fine seafood, cooking planks and seasonings (www.plankcooking.com), he's been planking for over 15 years and has demonstrated his techniques on "Martha Stewart Living Television," the CBS "Early Morning Show" and Food Network's "Best of," to name a few. John has generously shared his signature planked salmon recipe with me. You can buy the delicious dry rub in this recipe through his website. You'll have some left over; it's a great grilling rub for fish, chicken or veggies.

For the dry rub:

2 tsp | 10 mL lemon pepper

1 tsp | 5 mL granulated garlic

1 tsp | 5 mL dried tarragon

1 tsp | 5 mL dried basil

1 Tbsp | 15 mL paprika

1 Tbsp | 15 mL kosher salt

2 tsp | 10 mL light brown sugar

For the salmon:

1 cedar plank, soaked overnight or at least 1 hour

four 6-oz | 175-g pieces of fresh salmon fillet, about 2 inches | 5 cm thick, skin removed

2 lemons, cut into 8 wedges

Combine the ingredients for the dry rub in a small bowl.

Place the fillets on wax paper. Sprinkle both sides of the fish evenly with 2 Tbsp | 25 mL of the dry rub, pressing the seasoning into the fish. Refrigerate, uncovered, for at least 2 hours and up to 12 hours.

Preheat the grill on medium-high for 5 or 10 minutes or until the chamber temperature rises above 500°F | 260°C. Rinse the plank and place it on the cooking grate. Cover the grill and heat the plank for 4 or 5 minutes, or until it starts to throw off a bit of smoke and crackles lightly. Reduce the heat to medium.

Place the salmon on the plank and cook for 8 to 10 minutes or until the fish has an internal temperature of 135°F | 57°C. (This temperature is my standard doneness measure for fish. Chef Howie prefers his salmon rarer and removes it from the heat at 120°F | 50°C.) Transfer the salmon pieces to plates and serve garnished with lemon wedges.

PLANKING
⪢ SECRETS ⪡

Make a bed on your plank for extra flavor. Place a bundle of fresh herbs, some chopped scallions or a handful of crushed garlic cloves on the plank before you put your meat or fish on to cook.

fred's CITRUS SALMON

Serves 6 to 8

Brian Misko is an enthusiastic barbecuer who recently took the plunge and started up a barbecue team, House of Q. Brian passed on this recipe, which he has cooked time and again for his family. "It was originally crafted after salmon fishing in Tofino with my in-laws," he says. "I had never been fishing on the open ocean before, nor had Fred Kraus, my father-in-law. Nonetheless, a nice side of salmon was decorated for the grill with whatever we had in the cabin." And they've cooked it that way ever since. "Serve with a wonderful fruity white wine and a salad, and you have a nice west coast meal," says Brian.

1 alder cooking plank, soaked overnight or at least 1 hour

1 orange

1 lime

1 lemon

1 tsp | 5 mL grated zest from the three fruits (optional)

2 cloves garlic, finely minced or pushed through a press

1/4 to 1/2 cup | 50 to 125 mL olive oil

kosher salt and freshly ground black pepper

1 whole, boned fillet wild Pacific salmon (about 3 lb | 1.5 kg), skin on

extra citrus fruits for garnish

Squeeze the juice from the three fruits into a nonreactive dish like a lasagna pan. Reserve a few slices for garnish. Don't worry about pulp or seeds in the marinade—it all adds flavor. Add the zest, if desired, and the garlic and oil. The volume of oil depends on how big your piece of salmon is. A larger one will take a bit more oil. Whisk together all the ingredients and pour over the salmon. Marinate for a minimum of 1 hour at room temperature.

Preheat the grill on medium-high for 5 or 10 minutes or until the chamber temperature rises above 500°F | 260°C. Rinse the plank and place it on the cooking grate. Cover the grill and heat the plank for 4 or 5 minutes, or until it starts to throw off a bit of smoke and crackles lightly. Reduce the heat to medium-low.

Remove the salmon from the marinade and season it with salt and pepper. Place it on the plank and cook for 15 to 20 minutes or until the fish has an internal temperature of 135°F | 57°C. Halfway through the cooking time, spoon some of the marinade on top of the fish. When the salmon is done, serve it on the plank garnished with extra citrus slices.

salmon with PESTO

Serves 6

This is another classic way to plank salmon. Serve with a tossed green salad and maybe some Fettuccini Alfredo (page 93).

For the salmon:

one 2¹/₂-lb | 1.2-kg boned salmon fillet, skin on

kosher salt and freshly ground black pepper

2 lemons, one for juice, one for garnish

1/2 cup | 125 mL extra virgin olive oil

For the pesto:

1 cup | 250 mL basil leaves, washed and dried

6 cloves garlic, peeled

1/3 cup | 75 mL pine nuts

1 cup | 250 mL grated Parmesan cheese

3/4 cup | 175 mL extra virgin olive oil

kosher salt and freshly ground black pepper

Cut the fillet into 6 even portions. Season on all sides with salt and pepper. Combine the juice of one lemon with the olive oil and pour it over the salmon. Let marinate at room temperature for about an hour.

In a food processor, purée the basil, garlic, pine nuts and Parmesan cheese with 2 or 3 Tbsp | 30 or 45 mL of the olive oil. With the processor running, slowly add the rest of the oil. Season with salt and pepper.

Coat the salmon pieces generously with the pesto (you'll have enough pesto left over to toss with some pasta another day; it freezes well, too).

Preheat the grill on medium-high for 5 or 10 minutes or until the chamber temperature rises above 500°F | 260°C. Rinse the plank and place it on the cooking grate. Cover the grill and heat the plank for 4 or 5 minutes, or until it starts to throw off a bit of smoke and crackles lightly. Reduce the heat to medium-low. Place the salmon portions on the plank, leaving room around each for heat to circulate. Cook for 8 to 12 minutes or to an internal temperature of 135°F | 57°C. Serve garnished with lemon wedges.

planked SALMON
WITH ROSEMARY AND BALSAMIC VINAIGRETTE

Serves 6

Rosemary and salmon are a classic combination. In this recipe the honeyed balsamic vinaigrette and brown sugar intensify the flavor of this dish. Excellent on a bed of Roasted Garlic Mashed Potatoes (page 96).

For the vinaigrette:

kosher salt and freshly ground black pepper

1 tsp | 5 mL granulated garlic

1 Tbsp | 15 mL balsamic vinegar

3 Tbsp | 45 mL extra virgin olive oil

1 Tbsp | 15 mL liquid honey

1 shallot, peeled and finely chopped

1 tsp | 15 mL. grainy mustard

1/2 tsp | 2 mL dried rosemary

For the salmon:

1 plank (cedar is nice but any kind will do),
soaked overnight or at least 1 hour

2$\frac{1}{2}$-lb | 1.2-kg boned salmon fillet with skin

3 or 4 sprigs of fresh rosemary

extra virgin olive oil for drizzling

1 lemon, cut into wedges

1 green onion, finely chopped for garnish

balsamic reduction (optional; see sidebar page 46)

Combine the vinaigrette ingredients in a bowl and mix thoroughly. Coat the salmon fillet with the vinaigrette and set aside.

Preheat the grill on medium-high for 5 or 10 minutes or until the chamber temperature rises above 500°F | 260°C. Rinse the plank and place it on the cooking grate. Cover the grill and heat the plank for 4 or 5 minutes, or until it starts to throw off a bit of smoke and crackles lightly. Reduce the heat to medium-low.

Place the rosemary sprigs on the plank and lay the salmon fillet on top of the herbs, skin side down. Cook for about 15 minutes, or until the internal temperature is 135°F | 57°C. During cooking watch for flare-ups and put them out with a spray bottle of water.

Take the plank off the grill and transfer to a heatproof serving platter, tenting loosely with foil. To finish, season lightly with a little more salt and pepper, drizzle with olive oil and serve each portion with a wedge of lemon and a sprinkling of chopped green onion. For an extra-fancy touch, dot the plate with balsamic reduction.

SALMON with CRAB sauce

Serves 4

Christine Hunt, who lives on beautiful Salt Spring Island, is a member of the Kwakiutl First Nation and the third generation of her family to fish the Pacific waters off the coast of British Columbia. She's also a great cook. Christine's recipe, which I've adapted for planking, is a rich, creamy combination fit for a special occasion. It's best if made with fresh crabmeat, but it's also delish with canned. This dish goes well with roasted potatoes and lightly grilled vegetables like Florida Grilled Zucchini (page 92) and Grilled Asparagus (page 90).

1 alder or hickory plank, soaked overnight

**1¹/₂-lb | 750-g salmon fillet, skin on,
cut into 4 pieces**

2 tsp | 10 mL lemon pepper

2 Tbsp | 25 mL butter

2 Tbsp | 25 mL flour

2 cups | 500 mL whole milk

4 oz | 125 g light cream cheese, cubed

**juice and finely chopped or grated zest
of 1 lemon**

1 green onion, thinly sliced

**1/4 lb | 125 g fresh crabmeat
(or a 4¹/₂-oz | 128-mL can, with juice)**

Season the salmon pieces with 1 tsp | 5 mL of the lemon pepper and set aside.

Preheat your grill to medium-high heat. Meanwhile, melt the butter in a saucepan over medium-low heat. Stir in the flour and cook for about 1 minute. Gradually whisk in the milk and add the remaining 1 tsp | 5 mL of lemon pepper. Cook, stirring often, until the sauce has thickened, about 12 minutes. Whisk in the cream cheese until it melts into the sauce. Stir occasionally to maintain its smoothness.

While the sauce is cooking, rinse the plank and place it on the cooking grate. Cover the grill and heat the plank for 4 or 5 minutes, or until it starts to throw off a bit of smoke and crackles lightly. Reduce the heat to medium-low. Place the salmon pieces on the plank. They'll be done in about 8 to10 minutes, or when they're springy to the touch.

When the salmon is nearly done, transfer to a plate and cover loosely with foil. (While the fish is resting you might want to quickly grill some veggies.)

Finish the sauce by adding the lemon juice and zest, green onion and crab (include the juices if using tinned). Plate the salmon pieces, spoon on the crab sauce and serve.

soy-maple SALMON

Serves 6

East meets North in this classic planking recipe based on one shared by e-mail pen pal Kim Peterson, which contrasts the classic sweetness of maple syrup with Asian flavors of ginger and soy sauce.

**1 cedar, alder or maple plank,
soaked overnight or at least 1 hour**

1 cup | 250 mL pure maple syrup

2 Tbsp | 25 mL grated fresh ginger

1/4 cup | 50 mL fresh lemon juice

3 Tbsp | 45 mL soy sauce

2 cloves garlic, finely minced

kosher salt and freshly ground black pepper

2¹/₂-lb | 1-kg salmon fillet, skin on

greens from 1 bunch green onions, chopped

Combine the maple syrup, ginger, all but 1 Tbsp | 15 mL of the lemon juice, soy sauce, garlic, salt and pepper in a small pot. Cook at a simmer until reduced to 1 cup | 250 mL, about 30 minutes. Let cool. Season the salmon with salt and pepper and coat it with about half of the sauce.

Preheat the grill on medium-high for 5 or 10 minutes or until the chamber temperature rises above 500°F | 260°C. Rinse the plank and place it on the cooking grate. Cover the grill and heat the plank for 4 or 5 minutes, or until it starts to throw off a bit of smoke and crackles lightly. Reduce the heat to medium-low.

Quickly place the chopped onion greens on the plank, reserving about 1 Tbsp | 15 mL. Place the salmon on the greens. Cook for about 15 minutes, or until the internal temperature is 135°F | 57°C. During cooking watch for flare-ups and put them out with a spray bottle of water.

Take the plank off the grill and transfer to a heatproof serving platter, tenting loosely with foil. Finish the remaining sauce by adding the reserved lemon juice and warming it up a bit. Drizzle the salmon with the sauce and serve immediately, garnishing with the reserved chopped onion greens.

TOJO-STYLE miso marinated SALMON

Serves 6

Hidekazu Tojo is the owner and chef of Tojo's restaurant, one of the world's most famous Japanese eateries. Ever eaten a California roll? Tojo invented it. His flavor and texture combinations are brilliant. Here, I've simplified and adapted one of Tojo's fish recipes for the plank. He uses sablefish fillets rather than the salmon called for here, but any rich, dense-fleshed fish would work well. You can find the ingredients in the Asian section of most big supermarkets or, of course, in Japanese specialty stores. This salmon goes well on a bed of Wasabi Mashed Potatoes (page 97).

1 cedar plank, soaked overnight or at least 1 hour

six 6-oz | 175-g salmon fillets

kosher salt

1/2 cup | 125 mL miso paste

1/4 cup | 50 mL mirin

1/4 cup | 50 mL sake

1 tsp | 5 mL sugar

1/4 tsp | 1 mL togarashi chili pepper or
cayenne pepper

1 tsp | 5 mL finely minced fresh ginger

1 Tbsp | 15 mL finely chopped chives

1/2 cup | 125 mL shredded daikon
(Japanese radish) tossed with a few drops
each of rice vinegar, tamari and mirin

Salt the fish pieces on both sides and place them in a nonreactive pan.

In a mixing bowl, combine the miso, mirin, sake, sugar, chili pepper and ginger; it will form a fairly thick liquid. Pour the marinade over the fish and turn to coat. Cover and refrigerate for at least 2 hours or overnight.

Preheat the grill on medium-high for 5 or 10 minutes or until the chamber temperature rises above 500°F | 260°C. Rinse the plank and place it on the cooking grate. Cover the grill and heat the plank for 4 or 5 minutes, or until it starts to throw off a bit of smoke and crackles lightly. Reduce the heat to medium-low.

Place the fish pieces on the plank and cook for 10 to 15 minutes or until the fish has an internal temperature of 135°F | 57°C.

When the salmon is ready, transfer it to a platter and tent with foil for 3 or 4 minutes. Garnish with the chopped chives and serve with a little pile of grated daikon on the side.

planked TANDOORI salmon
WITH FRESH PEACH CHUTNEY AND MINTED YOGURT SAUCE

Serves 6

My brother Allan shared this delicious, colorful, award-winning recipe with me, and I'm delighted to pass it on to you, adapted for the plank.

For the salmon:

1 alder or cedar plank, soaked overnight or at least 1 hour

2/3 cup | 150 mL olive oil

1 clove garlic, finely chopped

six 8-oz | 250-g salmon fillets

1 Tbsp | 15 mL tandoori powder or garam masala

salt (preferably *fleur de sel* or other coarse sea salt)

For the peach chutney:

1 Tbsp | 15 mL sugar

1/4 cup | 50 mL rice vinegar

4 medium peaches, peeled and cut into 1/4-inch | 1-cm dice

2 Tbsp | 25 mL finely grated fresh ginger

For the yogurt sauce:

1$\frac{1}{2}$ tsp | 7 mL honey

1$\frac{1}{2}$ tsp | 7 mL finely chopped fresh mint

pinch ground cumin

pinch turmeric

1 cup | 250 mL plain low-fat yogurt

kosher salt and freshly ground black pepper

In a bowl, combine the olive oil and garlic. Rub the mixture all over the salmon. Sprinkle with the tandoori powder or garam masala and season lightly with salt. Cover and refrigerate for up to 2 hours.

In a nonreactive saucepan over moderately high heat, dissolve the sugar in the vinegar. Bring to a boil and cook for 1 minute. Stir in the peaches and ginger and return to a boil. Reduce the heat and simmer, stirring frequently, until the fruit is softened, about 5 minutes. Transfer to a bowl.

In another small bowl, combine the honey, mint, cumin and turmeric. Whisk in the yogurt until blended and season with salt and pepper. Cover and refrigerate.

Preheat the grill on medium-high for 5 or 10 minutes or until the chamber temperature rises above 500°F | 260°C. Rinse the plank and place it on the grate. Cover the grill and heat the plank for 4 or 5 minutes, or until it starts to throw off a bit of smoke and crackles lightly. Reduce the heat to medium.

Place the salmon fillets on the plank, making sure there's some room between each for heat circulation. Cook for 10 to 15 minutes or until the fish has an internal temperature of 135°F | 57°C. Serve with the chutney and yogurt sauce.

planked SALMON pizza

Serves 4

My pal Reza Mofakham helps manage a hardware store and caught the barbecue bug a couple years ago. He's learned to master the Cadillac of charcoal cookers, the Big Green Egg, which is kind of a cross between a covered grill and a tandoor oven—which means you can plank salmon and cook pizza in it. This dish scored well in the open category at the Canadian National Barbecue Championships in 2005, and I think it'll score well with you, too. It's a tasty way to deal with leftover planked salmon. If you don't feel like making your own pizza dough, you can buy it frozen in most supermarkets.

For the pesto sauce:

2 cups | 500 mL fresh basil

1/4 cup | 50 mL freshly grated Parmesan

1/4 cup | 50 mL toasted pine nuts

2 cloves garlic

1 tsp | 5 mL kosher salt

1/2 tsp | 2 mL freshly ground black pepper

1/4 cup | 50 mL olive oil

For the dough:

1 Tbsp | 15 mL sugar

1½ cups | 375 mL lukewarm water or beer

2 tsp | 10 mL dry yeast

4¼ cups | 1.1 L all-purpose flour

1 tsp | 5 mL kosher salt

2 Tbsp | 25 mL oil

For the toppings:

1/2 lb | 250 g leftover planked salmon, broken into bite-sized pieces

1 Tbsp | 15 mL capers

1/4 lb | 125 g goat cheese

2 Tbsp | 25 mL sun-dried tomatoes, coarsely chopped

Place the basil, Parmesan, pine nuts, garlic, salt and pepper in a blender. Blend until smooth, slowly adding the oil in a stream until you have a smooth, light green sauce. Set aside.

If you're using a breadmaker, prepare the ingredients according to the instructions for making bread dough. If you don't have a breadmaker, dissolve the sugar in 1/2 cup | 125 mL of the water or beer, sprinkle the yeast over top and let it sit for about 5 minutes.

Place the flour and salt in a food processor. Add the yeast mixture and the oil, and turn on the machine. Pour the rest of the water or beer through the feed tube of the food processor while it's running. Blend just until the dough forms a ball on the side of the bowl.

Remove the dough and knead it on a lightly floured surface for a few minutes. Transfer the dough to a bowl and lightly oil the top. Cover the bowl with plastic wrap and leave it in a warm, draft-free area for about 40 minutes until it has doubled in size.

Preheat grill or oven to 375 to 400°F | 190 to 200°C. Press the dough evenly onto a lightly oiled pizza stone or pizza pan. Spread the pesto evenly on the dough and add the salmon, capers, goat cheese and sun-dried tomatoes. Bake the pizza for 15 to 20 minutes or until the crust is golden brown and the cheese is melted.

OTHER SEAFOOD

Plank-cooking works well with almost any kind of seafood, from delicate white-fleshed fish like basa to shellfish like clams and scallops. You can never go wrong with cedar and seafood, although other woods are also great.

planked shad OR whitefish

Serves 6 to 8

This is about as close as you're going to get to replicating the traditional shad planking of the U.S. East Coast. It's based on a recipe from *The Boston Cooking-School Book* by Fanny Farmer, 1918 edition.

1 plank, preferably oak, soaked overnight or at least 1 hour

two 1¹/₂-lb | 750-g shad or whitefish fillets, deboned, skin on

kosher salt and freshly ground black pepper

1/4 lb | 125 g butter

1 Tbsp | 15 mL chopped fresh parsley

1 lemon, cut into wedges

Season the fish with salt and pepper.

Preheat the grill on medium-high for 5 or 10 minutes or until the chamber temperature rises above 500°F | 260°C. Rinse the plank and place it on the cooking grate. Cover the grill and heat the plank for 4 or 5 minutes, or until it starts to throw off a bit of smoke and crackles lightly. Reduce the heat to medium-low.

Place the fish, skin side down, on the plank. Cook for 10 to 15 minutes, or until the internal temperature is 135°F | 57°C. Meanwhile, melt the butter over low heat in a saucepan and set aside. Brush the fish generously with the melted butter and garnish with parsley and lemon.

HOW TO CHOOSE AND STORE SALMON AND ➤ OTHER FISH ≈

When shopping for fresh fish, look for a place that goes through a lot of fresh fish! The faster the fish is selling, the more likely it is to be fresh.

Don't be afraid to buy frozen fish. Which would you rather eat—a fish that was caught in the open ocean and immediately frozen at sea, or one that was freshly caught and has been sitting on a boat, and then in a warehouse, and then in a store?

Thaw fish using cold water. Fresh-frozen fish can be thawed easily by placing it, still in its packaging, in a sink full of cold water. Half an hour in a water bath and the fish is thawed and ready to cook.

Look for firm, shiny flesh that smells as fresh as it looks. Touch the fish. It should be firm to the touch, with a nice sheen, and should smell fresh and not fishy.

Store your fish packed with ice. To keep fish at optimum freshness in your refrigerator, keep it in its sealed packaging and surround it with ice.

BASA fillets with QUICK MUSTARD-DILL SAUCE

Serves 4

Basa is a farmed fish from Vietnam that has the delicate texture of sole but with a larger fillet and a richer flavor. If you can't find basa you can substitute another white-fleshed fish like sole, pike, halibut or catfish. This goes well with Pauline's Wild Rice Salad (page 84).

1 cedar plank, soaked overnight or at least 1 hour

two 12-oz | 350-g basa fillets

kosher salt and freshly ground black pepper

**1 tsp | 5 mL dried dill or 1 Tbsp | 15 mL chopped fresh dill
(in this recipe I prefer dried dill because the flavor is more intense)**

1 Tbsp | 15 mL honey mustard

juice of 1 lemon

2 Tbsp | 25 mL extra virgin olive oil

lemon wedges for garnish

Cut the basa fillets in half to make 4 equal-sized pieces and season them with salt and pepper. In a bowl mix together the dill, mustard, lemon juice and olive oil.

Preheat the grill on medium-high for 5 or 10 minutes or until the chamber temperature rises above 500°F | 260°C. Rinse the plank and place it on the cooking grate. Cover the grill and heat the plank for 4 or 5 minutes, or until it starts to throw off a bit of smoke and crackles lightly. Reduce the heat to medium-low.

Put the fish pieces on the plank and cook for 10 to 15 minutes or until the fish has an internal temperature of 135°F | 57°C. Remove from the grill and serve immediately with lemon wedges on the side.

cumin-curry
BASA with BANANA-YOGURT SALSA

Serves 4

Basa is the tofu of the sea—it easily takes on flavors while retaining its succulent texture. Any white-fleshed fish will also work here. This dish goes nicely with plain basmati rice and Grilled Asparagus (page 90).

1 cedar plank, soaked overnight or at least 1 hour

two 12-oz | 350-g basa fillets

kosher salt

1 Tbsp | 15 mL curry powder

1 tsp | 5 mL light brown sugar

pinch cayenne pepper

1 Tbsp | 15 mL toasted cumin seeds

1 lime, cut in half

1 medium-ripe banana

1/2 cup | 125 mL plain yogurt

1 Tbsp | 15 mL chopped cilantro

cilantro sprigs for garnish

your favorite chutney

Cut the basa fillets in two to make four equal-sized pieces. Season them with salt and put them in a nonreactive dish or bowl. Mix the curry, sugar, cayenne and cumin together and lightly coat the fillets on both sides with the rub. Squeeze half the lime over the rubbed fish pieces. Refrigerate for at least 15 minutes but not longer than an hour.

Chop the banana into 1/2-inch | 1-cm chunks and combine in a bowl with the yogurt and chopped cilantro. Cover and refrigerate until ready to use. This should be made shortly before you serve it.

Preheat the grill on medium-high for 5 or 10 minutes or until the chamber temperature rises above 500°F | 260°C. Rinse the plank and place it on the cooking grate. Cover the grill and heat the plank for 4 or 5 minutes, or until it starts to throw off a bit of smoke and crackles lightly. Reduce the heat to medium-low.

Put the fish pieces on the plank and cook for 10 to 15 minutes or until the fish has an internal temperature of 135°F | 57°C. Remove from the grill, garnish with a sprig of cilantro and serve immediately with the banana-yogurt mixture and some chutney.

PLANKED TROUT with almond butter

Serves 4

Using foil to loosely enclose the trout on the plank helps it cook more evenly and preserves the juices of this delicate fish. The plank will still infuse it with flavor. You might call this plank/baking fusion, or perhaps just plain confusion. I call it tasty trout.

1 cedar plank, soaked overnight or at least 1 hour

1 cup | 250 mL slivered almonds

1/4 cup | 50 mL butter

1 Tbsp | 15 mL chopped fresh parsley

1 clove garlic, smashed or pushed through a press

1 lemon, halved

butter to coat foil

one 2-lb | 1-kg trout

kosher salt and freshly ground black pepper

granulated onion (onion powder will do)

lemon wedges and parsley sprigs for garnish

In a 350°F | 175°C oven, toast the almonds on a baking sheet until golden brown, about 10 minutes. Set aside 1/2 cup | 125 mL for garnish.

Combine the remaining 1/2 cup | 125 mL of the almonds with the butter, chopped parsley, garlic and juice of 1/2 lemon in a food processor and blend until smooth. (It keeps for a week or two in the fridge and indefinitely in the freezer; bring the almond butter to room temperature before using.) Tear off a strip of heavy-duty foil $2^1/2$ times the length of the trout and double it. Spread a thin coating of butter (dairy butter, not the almond butter) over the top surface of the foil. Place the fish on the buttered foil. Lightly season the fish inside and out with salt and pepper and a little granulated onion. Daub the almond butter all over the inside and outside of the fish. Squeeze the remaining lemon over the trout. Wrap the foil around the fish, taking care not to seal it tightly—you want the aroma of the cedar to penetrate it during cooking.

Preheat the grill on medium-high for 5 or 10 minutes or until the chamber temperature rises above 500°F | 260°C. Rinse the plank and place it on the cooking grate. Cover the grill and heat the plank for 4 or 5 minutes, or until it starts to throw off a bit of smoke and crackles lightly. Reduce the heat to medium.

Place the fish on the plank and cook for 10 to 15 minutes, until the fish is springy to the touch or has an internal temperature of 135°F | 57°C. To serve, open up the foil, transfer the fish to a warmed platter and pour the juices left in the foil over the fish. Garnish with the lemon wedges, parsley sprigs and the remaining toasted almonds.

Planked Mushrooms or Veggie Kebabs
with Tarragon Vinaigrette
page 55

Planked Brie with Roasted Tomato and Cherry Relish
page 56

Gazpacho with Plank-Smoked Tomatoes
page 62

Planked Asparagus and Prosciutto Bundles
page 67

Plank-Baked Stuffed Potatoes
page 70

Fred's Citrus Salmon
page 112

Mixed Seafood Grill—Tojo-style Miso-marinated Salmon,
Planked Prawns Pistou, and Planked Scallops
page 118, 130 and 66

**Saffron Halibut with Avocado
and Tropical Fruit Salsa**
page 138

Really Easy Planked Chicken
page 143

Plank-Roasted Prime Rib
page 158

**Beef Burger with Chile Butter Core,
Dressed with Chipotle and Roasted
Garlic Mayo and Guacamole**
page 160

Planked Pork Loin Roast with Whiskey-Apricot Glaze
page 166

Spice-crusted Pork Tenderloin
page 168

Asian Lamb Racks
page 176

Mission Hill Planked Peaches with Rhubarb Compote
page 192

**Planked Pears with Walnuts
and Blue Cheese**
page 194

PLANKED **clams**

Serves 2 as a main course or 6 as an appetizer

In a book about west coast First Nations cooking techniques, I saw the simplest recipe for bar-becued clams: "Place clams on the embers of a fire. When the shells are open they are done." This recipe offers a tiny bit more, but it's in the same spirit. This dish works just as well with live mussels.

NOTE: Because this dish uses fairly high heat and takes little time to cook, you don't have to soak the plank for very long. If you get a bit of flaring around the edges it will shorten the cooking time and add to the flavor. Just be sure to have your spray bottle handy.

2 cedar planks, soaked for at least 20 minutes

1/4 cup | 50 mL butter

1 clove garlic, peeled and smashed or finely chopped

1 lemon, halved

2 to 3 lb | 1 to 1.5 kg fresh live clams, washed and drained

2 Tbsp | 25 mL chopped cilantro

French bread

In a saucepan combine the butter, garlic and juice of 1/2 lemon. Cook, stirring, over medium heat until the butter is melted and the garlic just starts to sizzle. Remove from the heat and keep warm on the stovetop.

Preheat your grill on medium-high for 5 minutes. Rinse the planks and place them on the cooking grate, side by side, with at least 1/2 inch | 1 cm space between them. Close the grill and heat the planks for 4 or 5 minutes, or until they start to throw off a bit of smoke and crackle lightly.

Place the clams on the planks, keeping the heat on medium-high, and close the grill. After about 2 or 3 minutes the smaller clams will start to open. Check every minute or so and transfer the open clams to a bowl. (Discard any clams that don't open.) When the clams are all done, gently toss them with the butter sauce, sprinkle them with the cilantro and serve with the bread.

PLANKED PRAWNS pistou

Serves 4 as a main course or 12 as an appetizer

Pistou is the French equivalent of the Italian pesto sauce. In this version I've added toasted nuts, anchovies and lemon zest for an extra kick. It's great with prawns, and these jumbo skewers create a spectacular impression. This sauce also works well as a coating for roast lamb.

For the pistou:

1/4 cup | 50 mL lightly toasted pecans (almonds or pine nuts are also excellent)

2 cups | 500 mL loosely packed fresh basil leaves

1 cup | 250 mL loosely packed flat-leaf Italian parsley

12 anchovy fillets, rinsed

2 cloves garlic, peeled

1/3 cup | 75 mL extra virgin olive oil

zest of 1 lemon, finely grated or chopped

For the prawns:

1 plank, any kind you like, soaked overnight or at least 1 hour

twelve 6-inch | 15-cm bamboo skewers, soaked for at least 1 hour

12 jumbo prawns, in their shells

kosher salt and freshly ground black pepper

12 cherry or grape tomatoes

lemon wedges for garnish

Combine the pecans, basil, parsley, anchovies and garlic in a food processor and process until smooth. Add the oil slowly in a thin stream while the processor is running. Transfer the pistou to a bowl, add the zest and stir thoroughly. Transfer about 1/2 cup | 125 mL of the pistou to a serving bowl and reserve for dipping.

Season the prawns with salt and pepper. Toss them with the remaining pistou and refrigerate for 20 minutes or up to 1 hour. When you're ready to cook them, thread one prawn onto each skewer, with a cherry tomato threaded between the tail and the head.

Preheat the grill on medium-high for 5 or 10 minutes or until the chamber temperature rises above 500°F | 260°C. Rinse the plank and place it on the cooking grate. Cover the grill and heat the plank for 4 or 5 minutes, or until it starts to throw off a bit of smoke and crackles lightly. Reduce the heat to medium-low.

Place the prawns on the plank and cook for 2 to 3 minutes per side, or until just cooked through. Serve with the extra pistou for dipping and garnish with lemon wedges.

PLANKING ⤳ SECRET ⤳

Don't marinate fish too long in strongly acidic marinades, or it will literally cook. Acid breaks down the proteins in fish in the same way as heat. So if you keep fish in very acidic marinades for much longer than 15 minutes it will start to cook. That's fine if you want to make ceviche, but not good if you're planking or grilling the fish.

ted's PLANKED sea bass
WITH CUBAN MOJITO SAUCE

Serves 8

This recipe from Ted Reader's ground-breaking *Sticks & Stones* cookbook is outrageously good. It also works very well with any firm, white-fleshed fish, like halibut or sablefish.

1 recipe Cuban Mojito Sauce (recipe follows)

2 cedar planks, soaked overnight or at least 1 hour

8 skinless sea bass fillets (6 oz | 175 g each, about 2 inches | 5 cm thick)

kosher salt and freshly ground black pepper

2 limes, halved

cilantro sprigs for garnish

Prepare the Cuban Mojito Sauce and cool.

Season the sea bass fillets with salt and pepper, place in a nonreactive dish and pour half of the sauce over the fish. Let marinate for 30 minutes.

Preheat the grill on medium-high for 5 or 10 minutes or until the chamber temperature rises above 500°F | 260°C. Rinse the planks and place them side by side on the cooking grate, leaving at least an inch | 2.5 cm between the planks. Cover the grill and heat the planks for 4 or 5 minutes, or until they start to throw off a bit of smoke and crackle lightly. Reduce the heat to medium-low.

Place the marinated fish fillets on the planks. Close the lid and bake for 15 to 18 minutes, or until the fish has an internal temperature of 135°F | 57°C. Check periodically to make sure the plank isn't on fire and use a spray bottle to extinguish any flames. While the sea bass is cooking, heat the remaining Cuban Mojito Sauce.

Before removing the fish from the grill, squeeze the limes over the sea bass. Carefully remove the planks from the grill and, using a metal spatula, transfer the sea bass to a platter. Serve immediately with warm Cuban Mojito Sauce. Garnish with cilantro sprigs.

Cuban Mojito Sauce

Makes approximately 1^1/$_2$ cups | 375 mL

1/4 cup plus 2 Tbsp | 75 mL vegetable oil

1 medium onion, diced

2 cloves garlic, minced

1 to 2 Scotch bonnet or red jalapeño chiles, seeded and diced

2 roasted red peppers, peeled, seeded and diced

2 Tbsp | 25 mL chopped cilantro

2 bay leaves

1 cup | 250 mL tomato sauce

kosher salt and freshly ground black pepper

granulated sugar and fresh lime juice to taste

In a medium saucepan, heat the oil over medium-high heat. Sauté the onion, garlic and chiles for 3 to 4 minutes until tender. Add the roasted red peppers, cilantro and bay leaves and continue to cook for 4 more minutes, stirring occasionally. Add the tomato sauce. Bring the mixture to a rolling boil, reduce the heat and simmer for 15 minutes. Season with salt and pepper. Remove and discard the bay leaves.

Purée the mixture with a hand blender or food processor until smooth and thick. Fine-tune the flavorings by adding a pinch or 2 of granulated sugar and some squeezes of lime juice. Cool.

SWORDFISH kebabs

Makes 8 kebabs, enough for 4 lunch-sized portions or 8 hors d'oeuvres

This is a great light meal or appetizer, tasty and beautiful. The firm flesh of the swordfish holds up well on the skewer.

For the marinade:

1 Tbsp | 15 mL lemon juice

1 tsp | 5 mL finely chopped or grated lemon zest

1 Tbsp | 15 mL grainy mustard

2 Tbsp | 25 mL extra virgin olive oil

1 Tbsp | 15 mL finely chopped parsley

1 Tbsp | 15 mL finely chopped capers

1 clove garlic, finely minced

1 Tbsp | 15 mL balsamic vinegar

splash white wine

freshly ground black pepper

For the kebabs:

2 cedar planks, soaked overnight or at least 1 hour

eight 7-inch | 18-cm bamboo skewers, soaked for at least 1 hour

two 8-oz | 250-g swordfish steaks, about 3/4 inch | 1.5 cm thick

8 grape or cherry tomatoes

8 pitted black California olives

8 giant capers (find these in gourmet food shops and Italian markets)

1 red onion, cut into 8 bite-sized chunks

lemon wedges and parsley sprigs for garnish

Combine the marinade ingredients in a nonreactive bowl. Set aside about 1/3 of the mixture in a separate container. Cut the swordfish steaks into 24 equal pieces (2 cuts lengthwise, 3 cuts across) and toss with the larger portion of the marinade. Marinate for 20 minutes to 1 hour, but no longer.

Assemble 8 skewers, alternating fish and vegetables (tomato-fish-olive-fish-caper-fish-onion).

Preheat the grill on medium-high for 5 or 10 minutes or until the chamber temperature rises above 500°F | 260°C. Rinse the planks and place them on the cooking grate. Cover the grill and heat the planks for 4 or 5 minutes, or until they start to throw off a bit of smoke and crackle lightly. Reduce the heat to medium.

Place the kebabs on the planks. Cook for 12 to 15 minutes, turning once or twice, or until the fish chunks are springy to the touch. Season with a sprinkle of salt and serve with some of the reserved marinade drizzled over. Garnish with lemon wedges and a few parsley sprigs.

HALIBUT kebabs

Makes 8 kebabs, enough for 2 lunch-sized portions or 8 hors d'oeuvres

Halibut's firm, perfectly white flesh makes it spectacular in any recipe. I love these meaty skewers because they excite the eye and the palate with festive colors and tropical flavors.

For the marinade:

juice of 1 lime

2 Tbsp | 25 mL vegetable oil

2 Tbsp | 25 mL chopped fresh basil

1 clove garlic, finely minced

1/2 tsp | 2 mL dried red chili flakes (or to taste)

For the fish:

1 cedar plank, soaked overnight or at least 1 hour

1-lb | 500-g boneless, skinless halibut fillet, about 3/4 inch | 1.5 cm thick

twelve 7-inch | 18-cm bamboo skewers, soaked for at least 1 hour

2 ripe mangoes, peeled, pitted and cut into 12 bite-sized chunks

half a ripe pineapple, peeled, cored and cut into 12 bite-sized chunks

1 red onion, cut into 12 bite-sized chunks

kosher salt and freshly ground black pepper

olive oil for drizzling

lime wedges and basil sprigs for garnish

Combine the marinade ingredients in a nonreactive bowl. Cut the halibut into 24 equal pieces (2 cuts lengthwise, 3 cuts across) and toss with the marinade. Marinate for 20 minutes to 1 hour, but no longer.

Assemble 12 skewers, alternating chunks of fish and vegetables with the mango and pineapple (mango-fish-pineapple-fish-onion-fish).

Preheat the grill on medium-high for 5 or 10 minutes or until the chamber temperature rises above 500°F | 260°C. Rinse the planks and place them on the cooking grate. Cover the grill and heat the planks for 4 or 5 minutes, or until they start to throw off a bit of smoke and crackle lightly. Reduce the heat to medium.

Place the kebabs on the planks. Cook for 12 to 15 minutes, turning once or twice, until the fish chunks are springy to the touch. Season with a sprinkle of salt, a drizzle of oil and serve, 2 to a plate. Garnish with lime wedges and basil sprigs.

saffron halibut WITH AVOCADO AND TROPICAL FRUIT SALSA

Serves 4 to 6

I get my fish at Westlynn Meats and Seafood in beautiful Lynn Valley in the heart of British Columbia's rainforest. Mike works there and he knows his fish. His unusual recipe, which I've adapted for the plank, pairs the intense flavor of the spiced halibut with a cool tropical salsa. Substitute snapper for halibut for a stronger flavor. Cuban-style Black Beans (page 98) and rice go very well with this.

For the fish:

1 plank (cedar or fruitwood), soaked overnight or at least 1 hour

four 6-oz | 175-g halibut fillets

kosher salt and freshly ground black pepper

1 tsp | 5 mL ground cumin

1/2 tsp | 2 mL turmeric

pinch saffron threads, crumbled

pinch cayenne pepper

1 lime, cut in half

extra virgin olive oil

For the salsa:

2 cups | 500 mL diced tropical fruit (any combination of mango, papaya, kiwi, pineapple)

2 just-ripe avocados, pitted, peeled and coarsely chopped

3 Tbsp | 45 mL chopped cilantro

3 Tbsp | 45 mL chopped red onion

1 jalapeño chile, seeded and finely chopped

juice of 1 lime

pinch sugar

kosher salt and freshly ground pepper

Season both sides of the fillets with salt and pepper. Combine the cumin, turmeric, saffron and cayenne and sprinkle lightly over the fillets. Squeeze the lime halves over the fillets and drizzle them with a little olive oil. Marinate for 15 minutes.

Preheat the grill on medium-high for 5 or 10 minutes or until the chamber temperature rises above 500°F | 260°C. Rinse the plank and place it on the cooking grate. Cover the grill and heat the plank for 4 or 5 minutes, or until it starts to throw off a bit of smoke and crackles lightly. Reduce the heat to medium-low.

Place the fillets on the plank and cook for 15 to 20 minutes or until the fish has an internal temperature of 135°F | 57°C. Remove from the grill and tent lightly in foil. Let rest for 2 or 3 minutes while you make the salsa.

In a salad bowl gently toss the salsa ingredients. Taste and season with salt and pepper. Serve the fillets topped with a dollop of salsa.

rum and HONEY PRAWN SKEWERS

Makes 8 kebabs, enough for 2 lunch-sized portions or 8 hors d'oeuvres

The combination of rum, honey and fresh mint is a revelation in this simple, delicious dish. If you're going to have it as a main course, serve it next to some of Pauline's Wild Rice Salad (page 84).

For the basting sauce:

2 Tbsp | 25 mL chopped fresh mint

juice of 1/2 lime

1 jigger Appleton Estate dark rum

1/3 cup | 75 mL liquid honey

1 tsp | 5 mL Dijon mustard

2 tsp | 5 mL vegetable oil

kosher salt

For the prawns:

eight 7-inch | 18-cm bamboo skewers, soaked for at least 1 hour

1 cedar plank, soaked overnight or at least 1 hour

16 extra large prawns, peeled and deveined (with tails on)

kosher salt

lime wedges and chopped mint for garnish

In a bowl, whisk together the basting sauce ingredients. Drizzle about 1/3 of the sauce over the prawns, tossing to coat. Set aside the rest of the sauce.

Assemble 8 skewers with 2 prawns on each.

Preheat the grill on medium-high for 5 or 10 minutes or until the chamber temperature rises above 500°F | 260°C. Rinse the planks and place them on the cooking grate. Cover the grill and heat the planks for 4 or 5 minutes, or until they start to throw off a bit of smoke and crackle lightly. Reduce the heat to medium.

Place the kebabs on the planks. Cook for 8 to 10 minutes, turning and basting regularly, until the prawns are firm to the touch. Season with a sprinkle of salt and serve with some of the remaining basting sauce drizzled over. Garnish with lime wedges and a sprinkle of chopped mint.

POULTRY

Chapter 5

The thing to know about planking poultry is that it seems to work best with hardwoods rather than cedar. For some reason the astringent flavor of cedar just doesn't go with the delicate taste of chicken. But planking chicken on hickory or fruitwood gives it a classic smoky barbecue flavor, and the gentle heat of planking makes for juicy, succulent meat.

REALLY easy PLANKED chicken

Serves 6 to 8

One of the biggest challenges of championship barbecue is finding a way to cook chicken so the skin doesn't turn out rubbery. With grilling, particularly over direct heat, chicken skin crisps up nicely, but cooking on a plank you also run the risk of getting tough, inedible skin. This recipe is based on a technique some barbecue competitors use to get chicken skin that melts in the judges' mouths. The secret is the acid in the dressing, which softens the skin.

2 hardwood planks (hickory, maple or apple would be nice), soaked overnight or at least 1 hour

2 chickens, cut into pieces, or 12 chicken thighs

kosher salt and freshly ground pepper

1 bottle store-bought zesty Italian salad dressing

Season the chicken pieces with salt and pepper and place them in an extra large freezer bag. Add the Italian dressing and marinate overnight.

Preheat the grill on medium-high for 5 or 10 minutes or until the chamber temperature rises above 500°F | 260°C. Rinse the planks and place them on the cooking grate, leaving about an inch | 2.5 cm of space between them. Cover the grill and heat the planks for 4 or 5 minutes, or until they start to throw off a bit of smoke and crackle lightly. Reduce the heat to medium.

Place the chicken pieces on the planks, skin side up, leaving at least a little space between them to ensure good circulation. Cook for 25 to 35 minutes or until the internal temperature reads 160°F | 71°C. Transfer from the plank to a serving platter and tent with foil to rest for about 5 or 10 minutes. Serve with your favorite accompaniments.

PLANKING ~ SECRETS ~

Everyone has had to deal with chicken fat flare-ups and outright fires in their grill. Plank-cooking reduces the risk of fire in the grill but doesn't eliminate it. Remember that the lower the cooking temperature, the lesser the risk of fatty flames.

Planks give a great smoky flavor, but they don't produce grill marks. If you like, take your chicken off the plank a few minutes before it's ready, remove the plank and toss the chicken around on the cooking grate to crisp up the skin and create some flavorful caramelization.

Chicken thighs cooked with wood smoke will usually develop a smoke ring—turning the meat close to the outside a characteristic red color. Inexperienced guests can sometimes mistake this for underdone fowl. Reassure them by making sure you monitor the internal temperature of the meat during cooking and remove the chicken only after it has reached the desired 160°F | 71°C at its thickest part.

As an alternative to bottled Italian dressing, some barbecue competitors marinate their chicken in plain or seasoned yogurt, which also tenderizes the skin. When you're ready to put the chicken on, wipe off the yogurt, coat it with a light layer of prepared mustard and dust it with barbecue rub.

teriyaki CHICKEN thighs

Serves 2 to 4

The teriyaki sauce in this recipe is a bit fussy, and if you don't feel like that much rigmarole you can use bottled teriyaki sauce. Serve with stir-fried veggies and steamed sushi rice.

1 plank (fruitwood or hickory would work well here), soaked overnight or at least 1 hour

8 chicken thighs (I prefer the skin on and the bone in, but boneless and skinless also work fine)

1 cup | 250 mL Complicated but Delicious Teriyaki Sauce (page 35)

2 Tbsp | 25 mL toasted sesame seeds

1 green onion, chopped

Trim the excess skin and fat from the chicken thighs and place them in a large resealable plastic bag along with the teriyaki sauce. Refrigerate for 2 hours or overnight.

Preheat the grill on medium-high for 5 or 10 minutes or until the chamber temperature rises above 500°F | 260°C. Rinse the plank and place it on the cooking grate. Cover the grill and heat the plank for 4 or 5 minutes, or until it starts to throw off a bit of smoke and crackles lightly. Reduce the heat to medium.

Place the chicken thighs on the plank, skin side up, leaving a bit of space between the pieces for air circulation. Sprinkle them with a light coating of sesame seeds. Cook for 30 to 45 minutes, or until the internal temperature reaches 160°F | 71°C (boneless will cook faster). Garnish with chopped green onions and serve some teriyaki sauce on the side.

beer-can CHICKEN on a PLANK

Serves 4 to 6

Grilling guru Steven Raichlen made this cooking technique famous. Here's my take on it, using a plank. The beer can moderates the heat, so the chicken stays moist and succulent over the long cooking time.

NOTE: Planks, especially thinner, wider ones, tend to warp when preheated on the grill. Be sure to balance the chicken in the center of the plank, and take care in the first few minutes of cooking to keep an eye on your bird so that it doesn't keel over.

1 plank (hickory, oak and mesquite work well here), soaked overnight or at least 1 hour

1 large, whole free-range chicken (5 to 6 lb | 2.2 to 2.7 kg)

3 Tbsp | 45 mL Championship Barbecue Rub (page 29) or your favorite grilling rub

one 12-oz | 355-mL can beer

Trim the excess fat from the bird. Wash it under cold running water and pat it dry. Sprinkle 1/3 of the rub inside the bird and 1/3 on the outside. Drink half the beer and put the remaining rub in the can. (I'm not sure what this does, but that's what the recipe calls for!)

Preheat the grill on medium-high for 5 or 10 minutes or until the chamber temperature rises above 500°F | 260°C. Rinse the plank and place it on the cooking grate. Cover the grill and heat the plank for 4 or 5 minutes, or until it starts to throw off a bit of smoke and crackles lightly. Reduce the heat to low.

Shove the can inside the cavity of the chicken, taking care not to spill the beer. Sit the chicken in the middle of the plank with its legs tucked in close to the can. Cover the grill and cook for 1 1/2 to 2 hours or until the internal temperature at the thigh joint is 160°F | 71°C. Remove the chicken and transfer it, still with the beer can, onto a carving or serving platter. Let it rest for 5 minutes, then carve it right off the can, as it were, and serve.

championship barbecue CHICKEN

Serves 6 to 8

This recipe was first developed by my friend and fellow Butt Shredder, Ann Marie "Amo" Jackson, and it has won us some trophies over the years. The sauces are based on recipes by Paul Kirk, the one and only Baron of Barbecue. The key with this recipe is to cook at a low heat and baste often to keep the skin moist and tender. You'll have lots of barbecue sauce left over. It keeps indefinitely in the fridge.

For the chicken:

2 fruitwood planks, soaked overnight or at least 1 hour

2 medium-sized chickens (4 to 5 lb | 1.8 to 2.2 kg), quartered and backbones removed

1 recipe Asian Poultry Brine (page 36)

For the barbecue sauce:

2 cups | 500 mL ketchup

1 cup | 250 mL white vinegar

1 cup | 250 mL dark brown sugar, tightly packed

1/2 cup | 125 mL pineapple juice

2 Tbsp | 25 mL soy sauce

1 tsp | 5 mL kosher salt

1 tsp | 5 mL cayenne pepper or ground dried chipotles

For the chicken baste:

3/4 cup | 175 mL pineapple juice

juice of 1 lime

1/4 cup | 50 mL butter, melted

2 Tbsp | 25 mL soy sauce

2 Tbsp | 25 mL clover honey

1 Tbsp | 15 mL finely chopped fresh parsley

1 garlic clove, smashed or pushed through a garlic press

1/2 tsp | 2 mL kosher salt

Marinate the chicken with the brine in a nonreactive pot for 2 to 4 hours.

Make the barbecue sauce by mixing all the ingredients in a saucepan. Bring to a boil and then simmer for 15 to 20 minutes, stirring occasionally. Cool.

Make the baste by combining all the ingredients in a saucepan. Heat it just enough to melt the butter. Keep warm. It's best freshly made, but it can be kept in a nonreactive container for up to a week in the fridge.

Take the chicken pieces out of the brine and pat them dry. At this point you can sprinkle with a little barbecue rub, but it's not necessary.

Preheat the grill on medium-high for 5 or 10 minutes or until the chamber temperature rises above 500°F | 260°C. Rinse the planks and place them on the cooking grate, taking care to leave a space between the planks for good cirulation. Cover the grill and heat the planks for 4 or 5 minutes, or until they start to throw off a bit of smoke and crackle lightly. Reduce the heat to low.

Place the chicken pieces on the planks. Cover the grill and cook for about 1 hour, painting the chicken with the baste every 15 minutes, until the internal temperature at the thigh joint reaches 160°F | 71°C. Give the chicken a coat of the barbecue sauce and cook another 5 minutes. Transfer to a serving platter, tent loosely with foil and let rest for 5 or 10 minutes. Serve with some barbecue sauce on the side for dipping.

turkey BURGERS

Makes 5 or 6 patties

Every so often, out of the blue, I'll get an email from someone who is enjoying my first cookbook, *Barbecue Secrets*, and wants to share a recipe with me. Terry Kelly of Presque Isle, Maine, sent me this easy and delicious burger recipe created by his wife, Cathy, and I've adapted it for the plank. The delicate burgers work well on a plank because they don't stick, and you can give them a chance to firm up before you turn them.

1 plank (your choice), soaked overnight or at least 1 hour

1 to 1¹/₂ lb | 500 to 750 g ground turkey (15% fat)

1 egg

1/2 tsp | 2 mL freshly ground black pepper

1/4 tsp | 1 mL kosher salt

2 Tbsp | 25 mL bottled salad dressing (French or Catalina)

1 small yellow onion, finely chopped

1/2 tsp | 2 mL granulated garlic

2/3 cup | 150 mL Italian-style dry bread crumbs

cheese slices

burger buns

burger condiments—Terry likes sliced red onion, ketchup and Miracle Whip; Doctored Mayo (page 45) also works nicely

Mix the turkey, egg, pepper, salt, salad dressing, onion, garlic and bread crumbs together in a bowl and shape into 5 or 6 patties.

Preheat the grill on medium-high for 5 or 10 minutes or until the chamber temperature rises above 500°F | 260°C. Rinse the planks and place them on the cooking grate. Cover the grill and heat the planks for 4 or 5 minutes, or until they start to throw off a bit of smoke and crackle lightly.

Place the burgers on the planks. Reduce the heat to medium and cover the grill. Cook for 6 to 8 minutes, turn carefully, and cook another 6 to 8 minutes or until the burgers are springy to the touch. Put a cheese slice on each patty and cook another 2 to 3 minutes. Remove from the grill and serve immediately with your favorite burger fixings.

MEAT DISHES

Chapter 6

For me, backyard cooking is all about the meat, and plank-cooking offers the meat lover a way to infuse a roast, steak or chop with barbecue flavor, but with all the convenience of grilling. Planking is the doorway to a gentler approach to grilling meat. Use these recipes as a starting point for your own protein-heavy culinary adventures.

HIGH STEAKS PLANKING

First off, let me say that steaks and chops aren't natural choices for plank-cooking. We're used to grilling them, and we like the quick cooking and the charring that goes with tossing meat around on a hot grill. But planking brings its own rewards, particularly on gas grills, which lack the classic flavor of wood or charcoal. So I've developed a hybrid technique that takes the key elements of grilling and combines them with the benefits of plank-cooking.

1. Sear it on the grill before you place it on the plank. Just as your plank is almost ready for cooking, put the meat on the cooking grate next to the plank and sear it for a minute on each side. This gives you the char marks and some of the grilled flavor that you won't get on the gentler-cooking plank.

2. Choose thicker steaks or chops than you would normally cook on the grill. I'm talking about a cross between a steak and a roast. That way you can fit more meat on the plank, because in the world of planking, real estate is expensive. Cooking thin, wide steaks for 4 people can take 2 planks. Instead, cook thicker steaks and fit them on a single plank.

3. In some cases, you can finish the steak on the grill. This works when you want to apply a finishing glaze like a barbecue sauce, allowing you to increase the complexity and depth of the flavor by caramelizing the sauce and creating some charring.

4. Don't soak the plank as much. Experienced plankers aren't afraid of a little flame, or even a lot of flame, now and then. A plank that hasn't been soaked very long tends to flare around the edges, and this can help char and crisp the outer edges of your steak or chop.

5. Serve the meat sliced. Big, thick cuts look great when they're served pre-sliced, and they're easier to eat. Just be sure to let the meat rest for a few minutes before slicing to help preserve the juices.

6. Make good use of marinades and rubs to add flavor. Plank-cooking takes more planning and a little more work than grilling. Make it special by using interesting baths and coatings for your meat.

PLANKING ⮞ SECRET ⮜

The flavor of cedar smoke goes well with so many foods, from salmon to cheese, and even beef. But most of the time, when I'm planking beef, I want classic hardwood flavor. I choose planks made of oak, hickory and mesquite, although fruitwoods also work well.

BEEF tenderloin STEAKS
with gorgonzola butter

Serves 6

This is dead simple, and deadly delicious. Just make sure you don't overcook it! Serve with your favorite steak accompaniments like Grilled Asparagus (page 90) and Roasted Garlic Mashed Potatoes (page 96).

1 alder, oak or cherry plank, soaked overnight or at least 1 hour

six 6-oz | 175-g tenderloin (filet mignon) steaks, about 2 inches | 5 cm thick

kosher salt and freshly ground black pepper

olive oil

Gorgonzola Butter (page 43), at room temperature

Generously season the steaks with salt and coarsely ground black pepper. Let them sit for an hour to bring them to room temperature.

Preheat the grill on medium-high for 5 or 10 minutes or until the chamber temperature rises above 500°F | 260°C. Rinse the plank and place it on the cooking grate. Cover the grill and heat the plank for 4 or 5 minutes, or until it starts to throw off a bit of smoke and crackles lightly. Keep the heat on medium-high.

When the plank is almost ready, drizzle the steaks with a little oil and place them directly on the cooking grate for about 1 minute per side to get some nice char marks. Transfer the steaks to the plank and reduce the heat to medium. Cook the steaks for another 5 or 10 minutes (depending on how rare you like them), turning once halfway through the cooking time. Take the steaks out of the grill, tent them in foil and let them rest for a few minutes. Serve with a pat of the Gorgonzola butter.

T-BONE STEAK with rosemary and balsamic marinade

Serves 4

The key ingredient here is the balsamic reduction, which penetrates the steak and gives it a tangy, sweet flavor. This dish goes well with mashed or roasted potatoes and grilled vegetables.

1 hardwood plank (hickory, oak or mesquite are best), soaked overnight or at least 1 hour

2 T-bone steaks, 16 to 20 oz | 500 to 600 g each and about 2 inches | 6 cm thick

kosher salt

cayenne pepper

1 Tbsp | 15 mL chopped fresh rosemary

2 cloves garlic, smashed or pushed through a press

1/3 cup | 75 mL balsamic reduction (see sidebar page 46)

Take the steaks out of the fridge and put them in a nonreactive dish. Season them with salt and a pinch of cayenne on both sides. Evenly spread the rosemary and garlic over the steaks. Set aside half of the balsamic reduction and drizzle the rest over the steaks, turning to coat both sides. Refrigerate the steaks, uncovered, for at least 2 hours or overnight, turning once or twice.

Preheat the grill on medium-high for 5 or 10 minutes or until the chamber temperature rises above 500°F | 260°C. Rinse the plank and place it on the cooking grate. At the same time, place the steaks directly on the cooking grate. Cover the grill and cook for 2 minutes. Turn the steaks, close the grill and cook for another 2 minutes. Transfer the steaks to the plank, which by now should be starting to throw off a bit of smoke and crackling lightly. Reduce the heat to medium and continue to cook the steaks for another 10 to 15 minutes or until they have an internal temperature of 125°F | 52°C.

Remove from the grill and let rest, loosely tented in foil, for about 5 minutes. Remove the steaks from the bone and carve them into 1/2-inch | 1-cm slices. Divide the slices between 4 plates and drizzle with the remaining balsamic reduction.

plank-roasted **chateaubriand** À LA JAMISON

Serves 6 to 8

A few years back, Cheryl and Bill Jamison wrote what are probably the best home-smoking cookbooks, *Smoke & Spice* and *Sublime Smoke*. They are culinary demi-gods, and I'm honored that they shared one of their favorite planking recipes with me. This is from their latest triumph, *The Big Book of Outdoor Cooking and Entertaining*. The Jamisons' method differs slightly from mine, and I defer to them in this recipe.

NOTE: Chateaubriand, or filet mignon roast, is cut from the thickest portion of the beef tenderloin, a section generally about 3 inches | 7.5 cm in diameter.

For the Mexican Coffee Rub:

2 Tbsp | 25 mL coarse-ground coffee

2 Tbsp | 25 mL finely chopped nuts, such as hazelnuts or pecans

1 Tbsp | 15 mL coarse-ground black pepper

1 Tbsp | 15 mL cocoa powder

1½ tsp | 7 mL coarse salt, either kosher or sea salt

1/2 tsp | 2 mL ground cinnamon

For the roast:

1 plank, preferably cedar or maple (1/2 to 1 inch | 1 – 2.5 cm thick and long enough for the beef but short enough to fit inside your grill), soaked overnight or at least 2 hours

one 3-lb | 1.5-kg chateaubriand beef tenderloin roast

2 tsp | 10 mL vegetable oil

Prepare the rub, combining the ingredients in a small bowl. Coat the surface of the meat with oil and then pat it generously with as much rub as will stick. Let the beef sit at room temperature for about 30 minutes.

Preheat the grill on medium-high for 5 or 10 minutes or until the chamber temperature rises above 500°F | 260°C. Rinse the plank and place it on the cooking grate. Cover the grill and heat the plank for 4 or 5 minutes, or until it starts to throw off a bit of smoke and crackles lightly.

Keeping the grill at medium-high, transfer the beef to the plank. Cover the grill and cook for 14 to 16 minutes over high heat, opening the grill at the 5- and 10-minute marks to spray the plank lightly with water (try to avoid spraying the meat), then quickly closing the grill again. (You should see a light plume of smoke during the whole cooking process. If you see a billowing dark cloud emerging, or any other sign that the board is burning instead of smoldering, open the grill carefully and douse any flames with the spray bottle of water.)

Turn off or shut down the heat and let the beef sit in the covered grill approximately 14 to 16 minutes longer, so it can cook further from the residual heat. The plank helps shield the beef from the heat, making the cooking time longer than if you were cooking it directly. The smoke will darken the surface further, and the high heat will nicely crisp it, an effect enhanced by the coarse spices. You don't want to overcook a piece of meat this special. We prefer to take the chateaubriand off when it's in the rare to medium-rare range, 120°F to 130°F, checked with an instant-read thermometer stuck deep in the meat.

Place a baking sheet upside down on the work surface nearest the grill and carefully transfer the plank, with the meat on it, to the sheet. (I use two large spatulas; the Jamisons recommend washable heatproof mitts.) Spray the plank again lightly to help it cool. The bottom of the plank will be sooty, so be careful where you place it, even after it's cooled.

Definitely show off your chateaubriand on the plank before dividing it up. The easiest way to serve is to bring the plates to the plank. If you want to serve the beef at the table, cover the baking sheet with a washable large cloth napkin or other fabric that can be cleaned easily. Place the beef-topped plank over the napkin and arrange the whole thing in the middle of the table to serve.

plank-roasted PRIME RIB

Serves 6 to 8

This is a novel way to cook a classic cut of beef because it imparts an unexpected smoky flavor (even more unusual if you use a cedar plank). The key with cuts like this is to be careful not to overcook.

For the dry rub:

1 Tbsp | 15 mL granulated garlic (or garlic powder)

1 Tbsp | 15 mL granulated onion (or onion powder)

1 Tbsp | 15 mL freshly ground coarse black pepper

1 Tbsp | 15 mL dried rosemary

1/4 to 1/2 tsp | 1 to 2 mL cayenne pepper

For the roast:

1 plank of your choice, soaked overnight or at least 1 hour

one 5-lb | 2.2-kg rib roast, bones attached

kosher salt

2 Tbsp | 25 mL. Dijon mustard

1 Tbsp | 15 mL coarsely chopped fresh rosemary leaves

extra virgin olive oil

4 or 5 whole rosemary branches, 5 inches | 12 cm long

Combine all the rub ingredients and set aside.

Take the roast out of the fridge and let it sit for an hour to come to room temperature. Season on all sides with kosher salt. Coat with the mustard. Sprinkle the rosemary evenly on the roast, then sprinkle generously with the dry rub (you'll have some left over). Drizzle with olive oil and pat the rub and rosemary into the roast.

Preheat the grill on medium-high for 5 or 10 minutes or until the chamber temperature rises above 500°F | 260°C. Rinse the plank and place it on the cooking grate. Cover the grill and heat the plank for 4 or 5 minutes, or until it starts to throw off a bit of smoke and crackles lightly. Reduce the heat to medium-low.

Lay the rosemary twigs across the plank to make a bed for the roast. Place the roast on the rosemary and cover the grill. Cook for $1^{1}/2$ to 2 hours, until the core of the roast reaches an internal temperature of 125°F | 52°C. Remove from the grill, tent loosely in foil and let rest for half an hour to an hour before serving with your favorite sides. (The long resting time gives you plenty of time to grill some veggies.)

BEEF BURGER with CHILE BUTTER CORE,

DRESSED WITH CHIPOTLE AND ROASTED GARLIC MAYO AND GUACAMOLE

Makes 4 large burgers

DISCLAIMER: This isn't a simple recipe and involves quite a bit of prep work. The chile butter and mayo need to be made in advance, so a little planning is necessary. Stuffing a disk of flavored butter into the burger patties takes a little practice, but the result will blow your guests away. The recipe was developed for the grill but takes well to plank-cooking. Be sure not to turn the burgers until they've started to get firm, and keep an eye out for flare-ups.

NOTE: Ground meat is best, and safest, when cooked on the same day it is ground. Get to know your butcher and ask for freshly ground chuck, which has the best flavor for burgers.

For the chile butter:

1/2 lb | 250 g butter

2 chipotle chiles in adobo sauce

2 Tbsp | 25 mL ancho chile powder

1 head roasted garlic (see sidebar page 43)

1/2 tsp | 2 mL salt

For the guacamole:

2 large ripe but still firm avocados

2 ripe tomatoes

juice of 2 limes or 1 lemon

1 clove garlic, finely minced

2 Tbsp | 25 mL chopped cilantro

3 tinned green chiles, rinsed, seeded and chopped

1 finely minced jalapeño or serrano chile (optional)

kosher salt

For the burgers:

1 plank (preferably oak, hickory or mesquite, but any hardwood will do), soaked overnight or at least 1 hour

1½ to 2 lb | 750 g to 1 kg ground beef
(20% fat)

1/4 cup | 50 mL cold water

1/2 tsp | 2 mL garlic salt

1/2 tsp | 2 mL onion salt

1 Tbsp | 15 mL prepared mustard

granulated garlic

Championship Barbecue Rub (page 29)
or your favorite grilling rub

1/4 cup | 50 mL Margie's Chipotle
and Roasted Garlic Mayo (page 45)

4 slices Jack cheese (optional)

4 hamburger buns

To make the chile butter, combine all the ingredients in a food processor and blend until smooth. Transfer onto a sheet of plastic wrap and shape into a tube 1½ inches | 4 cm in diameter. Twist the ends of the tube to close, and place in the freezer for at least 2 hours, and preferably overnight. (It's a good idea to make the mayo at the same time as you make the chile butter, as both improve when you let the flavors marry.)

To make the guacamole, peel the avocados and remove the pits. Coarsely chop the tomatoes and avocados. (You can mash the avocados as much as you like, but I prefer a chunky guacamole.) Blend in lime or lemon juice, garlic, chopped cilantro, green chiles and hot chiles, if desired. Season to taste with salt. This doesn't keep well and should be made no more than an hour before you put the burgers on the grill.

continues on next page ...

In a nonreactive bowl, combine the ground beef, water, garlic salt and onion salt. Mix lightly with your hands, being careful not to overwork the beef. Split into 4 equal portions and roll into balls. Take the chile butter out of the freezer and slice off four 1/4-inch | 0.5-cm disks. Poke your thumb in the middle of each ball to create a hole and insert the disk of chile butter. Encase the butter in the burger as you shape it into a classic burger shape about 3/4 inch | 1.2 cm thick, ensuring that there are no openings where molten butter could run out. Set the rest of the chile butter aside to soften.

Coat the burger patties lightly with mustard and sprinkle them with a light coating of granulated garlic, then a light coating of the rub.

Preheat the grill on medium-high for 5 or 10 minutes or until the chamber temperature rises above 500°F | 260°C. Rinse the plank and place it on the cooking grate. Cover the grill and heat the plank for 4 or 5 minutes, or until it starts to throw off a bit of smoke and crackles lightly. Reduce the heat to medium.

Brush the plank with a little vegetable oil and place the burgers on the plank (they'll be pretty crowded but should just fit). Cover the grill and cook for about 10 minutes, keeping an eye out for flare-ups. Turn carefully, and cook for another 10 to 15 minutes or until the patties become firm, but not hard, to the touch. If you want to add cheese, place a slice on top of each patty about 2 minutes before you plan to take them off the grill.

Transfer the burgers from the grill to a serving platter and remove the plank from the grill. Tent the burgers with foil and let rest for 2 or 3 minutes. In the meantime, coat the cut side of each half of the buns with some softened chile butter, sprinkle with a little granulated garlic and toast them for 30 to 60 seconds on the grill.

Dress the buns with a generous slather of chipotle mayo. Place the burgers on the buns and cover the burger with a big dollop of guacamole. Cover with the top half of the buns and serve.

NOTE: Warn your guests that the burgers have a molten filling or they could be in for a shock! In any case have plenty of napkins at the ready. These are very juicy burgers.

beef short ribs
WITH ASIAN DRY RUB

Serves 4 to 6

I love short ribs because they have so much fat and connective tissue. With slow cooking and a little smoke, they transform into rich, succulent, fork-tender morsels of pure carnivore love. This dish goes well with steamed rice and steamed Chinese broccoli dressed with a little oyster sauce.

NOTE: These take 2½ hours to cook, so you'll need time and a full propane tank.

For the dry rub:

1 Tbsp | 15 mL kosher salt

1 tsp | 5 mL freshly ground black pepper

1 tsp | 5 mL granulated garlic

1/2 tsp | 2 mL ginger powder

1/2 tsp | 2 mL Chinese five-spice powder

For the ribs:

1 plank of your choice, soaked overnight or at least 1 hour

four 10-oz | 300-g pieces of beef short ribs, at least 2 inches | 5 cm thick

prepared mustard

vegetable oil

Asian Barbecue Sauce (page 41)

Combine the rub ingredients in a small bowl. Coat the ribs with a thin layer of mustard. Lightly coat with the rub and drizzle with a little oil, patting gently so the ribs are glistening. Set aside.

Preheat the grill on medium-high for 5 or 10 minutes or until the chamber temperature rises above 500°F | 260°C. Rinse the plank and place it on the cooking grate. Cover the grill and heat the plank for 4 or 5 minutes, or until it starts to throw off a bit of smoke and crackles lightly. Reduce the heat to low.

Put the ribs on the plank. Cover the grill and cook for 2½ hours. Turn the ribs once at the halfway point and be careful to watch for flare-ups. Half an hour or so before they're done, turn them again and coat with barbecue sauce. The ribs are done when the meat has come away from the bone and has a soft, jelly-like feel. Remove from the grill and let rest, tented in foil, for 10 minutes. Serve with more sauce on the side for dipping.

CIDER-BRINED **pork** CHOPS

Serves 6 to 8

These delicious chops conjure up Old World flavors and remind me of autumn leaves and apple pie. These are big chops, designed for cooking on the plank. Serve them whole if you're feeding big appetites, but in most cases it's best to cut them into juicy strips and divvy them up.

For the brine:

4 cups | 1 L apple cider

3¹/₂ cups | 875 mL water

1/2 cup | 125 mL kosher salt

1/2 cup | 125 mL tightly packed light brown sugar

3 Tbsp | 45 mL coarsely ground black pepper

3 bay leaves

2 cinnamon sticks

10 juniper berries, crushed

For the chops:

2 cedar, apple or maple planks, soaked overnight or at least 1 hour

six 8-oz | 250-g extra-thick-cut pork chops

1 cup | 250 mL Ron's Rich, Deeply Satisfying Dipping Sauce (page 38) or your favorite bottled sauce

Combine the brine ingredients in a nonreactive pot. Place the chops in the brine and marinate, refrigerated, overnight.

Remove the chops from the brine and dry thoroughly with paper towels.

Preheat the grill on medium-high for 5 or 10 minutes or until the chamber temperature rises above 500°F | 260°C. Rinse the planks and place them on the cooking grate. Cover the grill and heat the planks for 4 or 5 minutes, or until they start to throw off a bit of smoke and crackle lightly. Reduce the heat to medium-low.

Place the chops on the planks and cover the grill. Cook for 15 to 20 minutes or until the internal temperature of the chops is about 140°F | 60°C. To finish the chops, remove them from the planks and transfer them to the cooking grate, taking the planks out of the grill at the same time. Coat the chops with barbecue sauce and turn up the heat. Place the meat on the hot grill for 2 or 3 more minutes, continuing to baste so the sauce becomes nicely sticky and caramelized. Remove from the grill, tent for a few minutes in foil and serve.

planked PORK LOIN ROAST
with whiskey-apricot glaze

Serves 4 to 6

In this recipe the aromatic, spicy, mildly astringent flavor of the cedar smoke nicely complements the pork's sweetness and richness. The trick with plank-cooking a roast this big is to get
the plank smoldering on high or medium-high heat and then turn it down to medium as soon
as you get the meat on. Serve slices of the pork with roasted vegetables on the side and, if you
like, some Roasted Garlic Mashed Potatoes (page 96).

1 cedar cooking plank, soaked overnight or at least 1 hour

one 14-oz | 398-mL can apricot halves in light syrup

1/4 cup | 50 mL Dijon mustard

1/4 cup | 50 mL Jack Daniel's whiskey

1/4 cup | 50 mL brown sugar

1/4 cup | 50 mL apricot jam

pinch cayenne pepper

one 3-lb | 1.5-kg pork loin roast with a 1/8-inch | 3-mm fat cap

kosher salt and freshly ground black pepper

sprigs fresh parsley and thyme for garnish

Open the can of apricots and drain the syrup into a medium-sized saucepan, reserving the fruit. Add the mustard, Jack Daniel's, brown sugar, apricot jam and cayenne to the syrup. Over medium heat, bring the mixture to a low boil, stirring to melt the sugar and the jam. When it looks like a smooth, fairly thick sauce (about 5 minutes), take it off the heat and set the pan in a bowl of ice cubes to cool.

With a sharp knife, lightly score the fat cap of the pork loin in a diamond pattern. Season it with salt and pepper, and set the meat on a sheet of heavy-duty aluminum foil. Spoon half of the mustard-whiskey mixture over the loin and pat it all over to coat. Wrap the foil around the meat, sealing it as best you can. Place the wrapped loin in the meat drawer of your fridge. Let it sit for a couple of hours at least, overnight if possible.

Combine the remaining half of the sauce with the reserved apricot halves, cover and refrigerate.

Preheat the grill on medium-high for 5 or 10 minutes or until the chamber temperature rises above 500°F | 260°C. Rinse the plank and place it on the cooking grate. Cover the grill and heat the plank for 4 or 5 minutes, or until it starts to throw off a bit of smoke and crackles lightly. Reduce the heat to medium-low.

Place the marinated pork loin on the plank fat side up. Cover the grill and cook for 1 hour, checking periodically for flare-ups.

At the one-hour mark, take the reserved apricots out of the sauce mixture and place them on the plank next to the roast. Baste the roast with some of the sauce and cook for another 10 or 20 minutes, until the internal temperature of the roast reaches 140°F | 60°C. Take the roast off the heat and lightly tent it in foil.

Transfer the apricot halves to a cutting board and coarsely chop them. Warm the remaining sauce on the stovetop or in the microwave and add the chopped apricots. Let the roast rest for at least 15 minutes (while it's resting, roast some vegetables on the grill). Carve the roast into 1/2-inch | 1-cm slices and serve on warmed plates with a spoonful of the apricots and sauce. Garnish with sprigs of parsley and thyme.

PLANKS AND PORK TENDERLOIN: THE PERFECT MARRIAGE

When I set out to research this book I knew that planking worked great for fish and for summer fruits like peaches and pears, but I had no idea what a perfect match this cooking style is for pork tenderloin. These little cylinders of tender, juicy pork are a staple of Chinese cooking and are wonderful on the grill, but they're also ideally suited to planking. Their size allows 2 or 3 to fit nicely on a plank, and they have just the right amount of surface area to cook quickly without losing moisture. They go with all flavors of smoke, from cedar to mesquite. And they take to marinades and rubs extremely well. Here are some basic techniques and a little collection of ideas for how to flavor pork tenderloin, but use your imagination and experiment with your favorite rubs, marinades and basting sauces.

Technique

1. Marinate and/or rub the tenderloin and have it ready to go before you start the grill. (Three tenderloins is usually enough for 4 servings.)

2. Preheat the grill on medium-high for 5 or 10 minutes or until the chamber temperature rises above 500°F | 260°C. Rinse the plank and place it on the cooking grate. Cover the grill and heat the plank for 4 or 5 minutes, or until it starts to throw off a bit of smoke and crackles lightly.

3. Reduce the heat to medium and place the tenderloin on the plank. Cook for 10 minutes, turn, and cook for another 5 to 10 minutes, basting if you like, until the pork is springy to the touch or reaches an internal temperature of 140°F | 60°C. (This will give you juicy pork cooked to a medium doneness. The internal temperature will come up slightly when you let the meat rest.)

4. If you like, just before it's ready, you can move the tenderloin from the plank onto the cooking grate and char the outside, or caramelize it if it's coated with barbecue sauce.

5. Take the tenderloin out of the grill, tent it in foil and let it rest for a few minutes before serving. Carve the tenderloin into 1/2- to 1-inch | 1- to 2.5-cm medallions and apply whatever sauce or garnish is called for.

Tasty Tenderloin Treatments

Classic Barbecue: Coat with ballpark mustard, sprinkle with Championship Barbecue Rub (page 29). Cook on a hickory plank till nearly done and finish with a light glaze of Ron's Rich, Deeply Satisfying Dipping Sauce (page 38). Serve more sauce on the side.

Easy Asian: Marinate with Easiest, Tastiest Steak (or Anything Else) Marinade (page 44) and finish with a coating of Asian Barbecue Sauce (page 41).

Spice-Crusted: Season with salt and pepper, drizzle with oil and coat with minced garlic, toasted fennel and cumin seeds, and a little cinnamon. Serve with chopped cilantro and your favorite chutney.

Balsamic: Coat with balsamic reduction (see sidebar page 46). Marinate overnight. Sprinkle on some chopped fresh rosemary and granulated garlic. Serve with a drizzle of the balsamic reduction and some chopped fresh mint.

Harvest Time: Season with salt and pepper and coat with a rub made with light brown sugar, powdered ginger, a sprinkle of freshly grated nutmeg, a pinch of clove and a little cayenne pepper. Baste with melted apple jelly and serve with Plank-Baked Apples with Rum-Honey Sauce (page 186).

Southwestern: Flavor using the same seasonings as Spice-Crusted Pork Blade Steaks (page 170) and serve with some salsa and cornbread.

REAL barbecue PORK on a plank

Serves 2 to 4

For this recipe I pushed the limits of planking and succeeded in cooking up some real, southern-style barbecue. This recipe is for advanced plankers only, ones with lots of time on their hands to boot.

NOTE: If you're using a propane grill, make sure you have a full bottle of fuel.

1 hardwood plank (hickory or maple would be best), soaked overnight or at least 1 hour

4 hickory chunks, soaked in water for at least 1 hour

4 pork hocks or shanks

4 garlic cloves, cut into slivers

vegetable oil

kosher salt and freshly ground black pepper

Ron's Rich, Deeply Satisfying Dipping Sauce (page 38)

Pierce the pork hocks with a sharp knife and insert slivers of garlic beneath the skin. Coat lightly in vegetable oil and generously salt and pepper all sides.

If you're using a gas grill, before you start, place one hickory chunk in each corner, above the burners but below the cooking grate. (If you're working with a charcoal grill, you need only one or 2 chunks, and you can put them on the coals just before you put the plank on.) Preheat the grill on medium-high for 5 or 10 minutes or until the chamber temperature rises above 500°F | 260°C. Rinse the plank and place it on the cooking grate. Cover the grill and heat the plank for 4 or 5 minutes, or until it starts to throw off a bit of smoke and crackles lightly. Reduce the heat to as low as it can go.

Place the pork hocks on the plank. Cook for 6 hours, taking care that there are no flare-ups (at a very low temperature this shouldn't be a problem, but closely monitor the situation just in case).

Remove the meat from the plank. Let it rest, tented in foil, for 5 or 10 minutes. The meat at this point should be so tender it will separate easily from the bones and skin. Remove the meat and serve as is, with a little dipping sauce on the side, or shred it, mix it with some sauce and have a pulled pork sandwich. Woo hoo! Barbecue on a plank!

spice-crusted PORK BLADE STEAKS

Serves 6

I developed this as a conventional grilling recipe for the folks at *Food & Wine* magazine for their 2005 summer barbecue issue. I love pork blade steaks because they're inexpensive, extremely tasty and very hard to ruin.

The cumin seeds add an earthy tang and interesting texture to these rich, flavorful, chewy steaks. Serve them with your favorite summer sides (I like grilled asparagus and cherry tomatoes).

For the rub:

2 Tbsp | 25 mL powdered ancho chiles
(if you can't find ground anchos, any chili powder will do)

1 Tbsp | 15 mL granulated garlic

1 Tbsp | 15 mL granulated onion

1 tsp | 5 mL freshly ground black pepper

1 tsp | 5 mL ground chipotles (substitute cayenne pepper if you can't find ground chipotles)

1 tsp | 5 mL dried oregano

1 tsp | 5 mL dried parsley

For the steaks:

2 planks (cedar or hickory would work well), soaked overnight or at least 1 hour

1 Tbsp | 15 mL cumin seeds

6 pork blade steaks (8 to 10 oz | 225 to 300 g each)

kosher salt

2 Tbsp | 25 mL Dijon mustard (regular prepared mustard will also do)

extra-virgin olive oil

Combine the rub ingredients in a small bowl and set aside.

In a dry frying pan over medium heat, toast the cumin seeds until they're fragrant and just starting to turn light brown. Remove from the pan and set aside.

Generously season the blade steaks with salt. Using the back of a spoon or a basting brush, coat the steaks with a thin layer of mustard. Sprinkle the cumin seeds on both sides of the steaks and pat them in so they stick to the mustard. Sprinkle a generous coating of rub on the steaks and drizzle with a little olive oil. (You'll have rub left over, which is great for grilling just about anything.)

Preheat the grill on medium-high for 5 or 10 minutes or until the chamber temperature rises above 500°F | 260°C. Rinse the planks and place them on the cooking grate, leaving about an inch | 2.5 cm of space between them. Cover the grill and heat the planks for 4 or 5 minutes, or until they start to throw off a bit of smoke and crackle lightly. Reduce the heat to medium.

Cook for 10 to 15 minutes, turning once or twice, or until the steaks are springy to the touch. If you like, you can finish these steaks on the grill to get some nice char marks. Just move them from the planks to the cooking grate for the last few minutes of cooking. Remove the steaks from the grill, tent with foil and let rest for 5 minutes. Drizzle with a little olive oil and serve.

WARNING: These steaks have a lot of juice and fat in them, so be on the alert for flare-ups.

PLANKED rack of venison WITH BALSAMIC RASPBERRY GLAZE

Serves 4

I love venison, but I don't cook it often, and I've never cooked it on a plank. Till now, that is. My buddy and King of the Q, Ted Reader, shared this superb venison recipe with me, which pairs classic Mediterranean flavors with a tasty cut of game.

For the venison:

1 cedar plank, soaked overnight or at least 1 hour

2 Tbsp | 25 mL cracked black pepper

2 cloves garlic, chopped

1 Tbsp | 15 mL chopped fresh rosemary

1 tsp | 5 mL coarse salt

2 Tbsp | 25 mL olive oil

one 2-lb | 1-kg rack of venison, frenched (trimmed to bare the ribs, and the excess fat and tough silverskin membrane removed)

For the glaze:

2 cloves garlic, chopped

3 shallots, diced

2 Tbsp | 25 mL olive oil

1/4 cup | 50 mL balsamic vinegar

3 cups | 750 mL fresh raspberries

1 cup | 250 mL honey

2 sprigs fresh thyme

1 tsp | 5 mL each kosher salt and cracked black pepper

In a small bowl combine the pepper, garlic, rosemary, salt and olive oil. Rub all over the venison rack, pressing the spices so they adhere to the meat. Set aside.

Prepare the glaze. In a saucepan over medium heat, sauté the garlic and shallots with the oil for 2 to 3 minutes, until tender and transparent. Pour the balsamic vinegar into the pan to deglaze, scraping up the brown bits. Boil gently and continue stirring until the liquid is reduced by half. Add the raspberries and continue to cook for another 3 minutes, stirring and slightly mashing the raspberries to extract the juice. Add the honey, thyme and black pepper. Bring to a boil and remove from the heat. Cool slightly. In a blender or food processor, purée until smooth. Strain, season with salt and let cool. Set aside.

Preheat the grill to high. Place the venison rack on the plank. Place the plank in the grill and close the lid. Grill for 15 to 18 minutes for medium-rare, basting 2 to 3 times with the balsamic raspberry glaze. Remove from the grill and allow to rest for 5 minutes. Slice the rack into chops $1^1/2$ to 2 inches | 4 to 5 cm thick and serve, drizzled with the extra glaze.

tandoori LAMB kebabs

Serves 4

Tandoori paste is available in the Indian food section of most supermarkets, and it's a great thing to have in your fridge. It adds great flavor to chicken and lamb, and if you have the fore-sight to marinate the meat overnight, it also has a tenderizing effect. Serve these lamb kebabs with steamed basmati rice, a vegetable curry and your favorite chutney.

eight 7-inch | 18-cm bamboo skewers, soaked for at least 1 hour

1 plank of your choice, soaked overnight or at least 1 hour

1/2 cup | 125 mL tandoori paste

1/3 cup | 75 mL yogurt

juice of 1 lemon

3 Tbsp | 45 mL chopped fresh cilantro

one 3 lb | 1.5 kg boneless leg of lamb, cut into chunks

1 large Spanish onion, cut into bite-sized chunks

3 oz | 75 g butter

lemon wedges and cilantro sprigs for garnish

In a nonreactive bowl mix together the tandoori paste, yogurt, lemon juice and chopped cilan-tro. Add the lamb chunks and coat with the marinade. Refrigerate overnight if possible, or at least 1 hour. Thread the lamb chunks onto the skewers, alternating with pieces of onion.

In a small saucepan heat the butter just until melted. Set aside and keep warm.

Preheat the grill on medium-high for 5 or 10 minutes or until the chamber temperature rises above 500°F | 260°C. Rinse the plank and place it on the cooking grate. Cover the grill and heat the plank for 4 or 5 minutes, or until it starts to throw off a bit of smoke and crackles lightly. Reduce the heat to medium.

Place the kebabs on the plank and cook for 12 to 15 minutes, or until the lamb chunks are springy to the touch. Every 3 or 4 minutes turn and baste the kebabs with butter (be sure to have your spray bottle at the ready; the butter can cause flare-ups). Remove from the grill and serve garnished with lemon wedges and cilantro sprigs.

LAMB-HENGE
(lamb loin chops with hazelnut crust)

Serves 6

Lamb loin chops look like mini T-bone steaks. But when set on end and placed on a plank, they look like little Druid monuments. This is a great way to cook them because you get excellent heat circulation for perfectly done meat and golden brown crust. Serve with mint jelly and some roasted vegetables on the side. You can also use 3 lamb racks for this recipe.

1 plank, any kind you like, soaked overnight or at least 1 hour

12 lamb loin chops, cut extra thick (1^{1}/$_{2}$ to 2 inches | 4 to 5 cm)

kosher salt and freshly ground black pepper

1/2 cup | 125 mL extra virgin olive oil

juice of 1/2 lemon

4 cloves garlic, pushed through a press

1 Tbsp | 15 mL coarsely chopped fresh rosemary needles

3/4 cup | 175 mL hazelnuts

3/4 cup | 175 mL dry bread crumbs (Japanese panko works well)

1 Tbsp | 15 mL dried parsley

Season the chops with salt and pepper. In a bowl, mix together the olive oil, lemon juice, garlic and rosemary. Toss the lamb chops in it to coat. Refrigerate for 2 hours.

In a sauté pan, toast the hazelnuts over medium heat, stirring frequently, until they're golden brown. Transfer them to a plate and cool for 5 minutes. Place the nuts, bread crumbs and dried parsley in a food processor and whiz until the nuts are finely ground and incorporated into the crumbs.

Preheat the grill on medium-high for 5 or 10 minutes or until the chamber temperature rises above 500°F | 260°C. Rinse the plank and place it on the cooking grate. Cover the grill and heat the plank for 4 or 5 minutes, or until it starts to throw off a bit of smoke and crackles lightly.

While the plank is heating, work quickly to remove the lamb chops from the marinade and coat them evenly with the breading mixture. When the plank is ready, stand the chops, bone side down, on the plank, cover and turn the heat down to medium. Cook the chops for about 12 to 15 minutes or until they're springy to the touch. Remove them from the plank and let them rest, loosely tented in foil, for about 5 minutes before serving.

asian LAMB racks

Serves 4 as a main course or 8 as an appetizer

Too often we just reach for the mint or rosemary when it comes to lamb, when it also happens to be delicious with these Asian flavors. The inspiration for the recipe comes from food stylist and TV chef Nathan Fong.

For the marinade/sauce:

1/2 cup | 125 mL hoisin sauce

2 Tbsp | 25 mL smooth peanut butter

2 Tbsp | 25 mL soy sauce

2 Tbsp | 25 mL dry sherry

2 Tbsp | 25 mL fresh squeezed orange juice

1 tsp | 5 mL finely chopped or grated orange zest

1 tsp | 5mL finely chopped or grated fresh ginger

1/2 tsp | 2 mL toasted sesame oil

2 cloves garlic, smashed or pushed through a garlic press

1/2 tsp | 2 mL crushed dried red chile flakes

For the lamb:

1 cedar or fruitwood plank, soaked overnight or at least 1 hour

4 racks of lamb, frenched (trimmed to bare the ribs, and the excess fat and tough silverskin

membrane removed)

kosher salt

1/2 cup | 125 mL coarsely chopped dry-roasted peanuts

chopped green onions for garnish

Whisk together the marinade/sauce ingredients and divide into 2 portions. Lightly season the lamb racks with salt. Coat the lamb racks with one portion of the marinade and set aside the other. Cover the lamb and refrigerate for 2 hours or overnight.

Preheat the grill on medium-high for 5 or 10 minutes or until the chamber temperature rises above 500°F | 260°C. Rinse the plank and place it on the cooking grate. Cover the grill and heat the plank for 4 or 5 minutes or until it starts to throw off a bit of smoke and crackles lightly. Reduce the heat to medium-low.

Place the lamb racks on the plank in pairs, facing one another, so the ribs interlock like fingers. Cook for 15 to 20 minutes or until the lamb has an internal temperature of 125°F | 52°C. Remove from the grill and tent loosely in foil for 5 or 10 minutes. Slice into chops and serve garnished with the chopped peanuts and green onions.

planked LEG OF LAMB with red wine REDUCTION

Serves 4 to 6

Yes, you can plank a whole leg of lamb. And, surprisingly, cedar works very nicely, although any of the hardwoods, particularly apple or cherry, are also excellent. Serve with Rosemary Roasted Carrots (page 91), which you can cook on the grill next to the lamb during the last hour of cooking.

1 cooking plank, soaked overnight or for at least 1 hour

one 6-lb | 2.7-kg bone-in leg of lamb

kosher salt and freshly ground black pepper

extra virgin olive oil

16 cloves garlic

1 Tbsp | 15 mL mustard powder

12 sprigs fresh thyme

one 750-mL bottle Cabernet Sauvignon or other red wine

1 cup | 250 mL chicken stock

3 large shallots, finely chopped

Season the lamb leg with salt and pepper and drizzle some olive oil on it, using your hands to evenly coat the leg in the oil. Push 4 of the garlic cloves through a garlic press and spread the garlic evenly over the lamb. Dust the leg with the mustard powder and massage it into the flesh. Lightly crush the rest of the garlic cloves with the flat side of a knife.

Preheat the grill on medium-high for 5 or 10 minutes or until the chamber temperature rises above 500°F | 260°C. Rinse the plank and place it on the cooking grate. Cover the grill and heat the plank for 4 or 5 minutes, or until it starts to throw off a bit of smoke and crackles lightly. Reduce the heat to medium-low.

On the plank, make a bed of the crushed garlic and half of the thyme sprigs. Place the lamb leg on top, fat side up, and place the rest of the thyme sprigs along the top of the roast, patting them so they stick to the meat. Cook for about 1½ hours or until the lamb has an internal temperature of 125°F | 52°C at the thickest part of the roast.

While the lamb is roasting, pour the wine and chicken stock into a heavy saucepan and add the shallots. Bring to a low boil and reduce until you have about a cupful of syrupy sauce. Set aside and keep warm.

When the lamb reaches the target internal temperature, take it off the grill and tent it loosely with foil. Let it rest for 30 to 45 minutes. Carve the lamb at the table and pass the sauce around.

BOARD OF DESSERTS
Fabulous Finales

Chapter 7

In this section you'll find a mix of unusual planked desserts as well as a selection of non-planked favorites from my wife, Kate, whose superb dessert recipes also graced the pages of *Barbecue Secrets*. A word to the wise: when you first start plank-cooking it's fun to serve whole menus with planked appetizers, main courses and desserts. But after a while it's good to break things up. Consider serving a more conventional dessert with a planked meal, and a planked dessert with a more conventional meal to give your guests some variety.

BLACK AND BLUE berries with lime ZEST CONFIT

Serves 6 to 8

This one's inspired by a dessert from celebrity chef Anthony Bourdain, who has "Blueberries with Lime Sugar" on the menu at Les Halles restaurant in New York. It's great with just blueberries, but my wife, Kate, decided it would benefit from the addition of blackberries. The combination works beautifully and kids love it, too. Don't forget to drink the juice!

For the lime zest confit:

2 limes

1 cup | 250 mL water

1/2 cup | 125 mL sugar

For the berries:

3 Tbsp | 45 mL sugar

juice of 2 limes

3/4 pint | 375 g fresh blueberries

3/4 pint | 375 g fresh blackberries

several sprigs fresh mint, finely chopped

1/2 cup | 125 mL crème fraîche or sour cream (optional)

To make the confit, remove the peel from the limes with a paring knife, being sure not to include the white pith. Slice the peel into thin pieces. (It's much easier to do this if you use a zester, which is a wonderful tool for all kinds of reasons.)

Combine the water and sugar in a small saucepan and bring the mixture to a boil. Add the zest and reduce the heat so the mixture simmers. Loosely cover the pot and let the liquid cook until it has reduced by half. Remove from the heat, cool it completely and strain. You can store the confit in an airtight container and refrigerate it until you need it.

To finish the dish, combine the sugar with the lime juice in a large, presentable bowl and stir to dissolve the sugar. Add the berries and toss them well, coating all the berries with the mixture. Add the fresh mint and the lime zest confit and toss it well again. The mixture is even better after the flavors have had time to marry, so refrigerate for an hour or more. Garnish with more fresh mint and serve with crème fraîche or sour cream, if you like.

PAVLOVA

Serves 8

This classic is one of my family's favorite party desserts. It contains no flour, which is great for your gluten-intolerant friends, and can be tarted up with almost any combination of fresh fruit. Mangoes and strawberries and grapes, for instance, with pomegranate seeds sprinkled over top. It's best to make pavlova when the weather is dry, so the meringue doesn't lose its delicious crunch. The lemon curd is definitely not required, but it adds welcome tang.

scant 3/4 cup | 175 mL egg whites (from 5 large eggs), completely yolk-free, at room temperature

1/4 tsp | 1 mL cream of tartar

pinch salt

5 tsp | 25 mL cornstarch, plus more for the baking sheet

1 2/3 cups | 400 mL granulated sugar

2 tsp | 10 mL white vinegar

1 tsp | 5 mL vanilla extract

2 cups | 500 mL whipping cream, chilled

1 Tbsp | 15 mL honey (optional)

1/2 cup | 125 mL Lemon Curd (optional; recipe follows)

3 cups | 750 mL (or so) cut-up fresh fruit or berries

mint sprigs for garnish (optional)

Position the oven rack a little below the middle of the oven. If your oven is electric, put a shallow pan of water on the bottom rack of the oven. Preheat the oven to 275°F | 140°C.

Line a baking sheet with cooking parchment (foil also works) and dust the sheet with cornstarch to make sure the meringue doesn't stick.

Warm a large, stainless steel bowl under hot water, then dry it thoroughly. Add the egg whites, cream of tartar and salt. Surround the bowl with a warm, damp dish towel to make sure the egg whites stay warm.

Combine the cornstarch with 2 Tbsp | 25 mL of the sugar and set it aside. Whip the egg white mixture at medium-high speed until it's stiff and starts to pull away from the sides of the bowl. Immediately begin adding the remaining sugar by sprinkling it into the egg whites slowly, a tablespoon at a time. Then add the cornstarch and sugar mixture. Scrape down the sides of the bowl and keep whipping, slowly adding the white vinegar and vanilla. Continue whipping for 1 minute more. At this point, the mixture should be glossy.

For individual pavlovas, use an cream scoop and stack 2 scoops together, then use the back of the scoop to sculpt each meringue into a volcano with a depression in the center.

For a large pavlova, use a spatula or spoon to spread the meringue into a 7-inch | 18-cm round, about 3 inches | 8 cm high, making a shallow depression in the middle. Feel free to give the edges some swirls.

Put the meringue in the heated oven and immediately reduce the heat to 250°F | 120°C. It's important that you don't open the door of the oven for at least 45 minutes (less for the smaller meringues). The meringue should be crisp and dry-looking. Bake the large meringues $1^{1}/_{2}$ hours; bake the smaller, 1 to $1^{1}/_{4}$ hours. Leave the meringues in the oven, with the heat turned off and the oven door cracked open, for another 30 minutes after baking. Then remove them from the oven and set the baking sheet on a rack to cool.

You can assemble the pavlova up to an hour before serving. Any more and it will start to get soggy. Whip the chilled cream until it holds soft peaks. Add the honey, if you're using it, and whip it another few seconds to blend it in. The cream should be holding slightly firmer peaks. Then, if you're using the lemon curd, fold it in gently. (Don't use too much!) Fill the center of the pavlova with the cream and gently top it with fruit. Keep cool. Serve garnished with mint sprigs, if desired.

Lemon Curd
Makes 1 pint | 500 mL

This is Martha Stewart's recipe, but you can find lemon curd recipes in lots of cookbooks. (You can also buy it.) Try it on warm gingerbread or scones.

6 egg yolks, lightly beaten

1 cup | 250 mL sugar

1/2 cup | 125 mL freshly squeezed lemon juice

1/4 lb | 125 g butter, cut into small pieces

1 Tbsp | 15 mL grated or finely minced lemon zest

Strain the egg yolks through a sieve into a medium, nonreactive saucepan. Place the pan over medium heat and stir in the sugar and lemon juice. Cook the mixture, stirring constantly, for 10 to 12 minutes. The mixture should thicken and coat the back of a wooden spoon. Make sure it doesn't boil.

Remove it from the heat and whisk it until it's slightly cooled, then stir in the butter a piece at a time. Add the zest. If you want to keep the curd for some time, pour it into hot, sterilized jars and cover them tightly. Once they've cooled, the jars of curd should be refrigerated until you want to break into them. Sterilized curd keeps for months.

TEXAS gold cookies

Makes 12 to 24 cookies, depending on their size

This decadent cookie recipe comes from the Upper Crust Bakery of Austin, Texas. It takes more time than your typical cookie batter, and it takes a heckuvalot more chocolate. The results speak for themselves. Have a glass of cold milk at the ready. (The Upper Crust uses 1/2 cup | 125 mL of dough for each of its cookies but also offers them in "cocktail size." The smaller versions, made from heaping tablespoons of dough, suit those of us who love to eat but aren't from Texas.)

3 oz | 75 g unsweetened chocolate, coarsely chopped

18 oz | 550 g semisweet chocolate, coarsely chopped

1/2 cup | 125 mL plus 1 Tbsp | 15 mL unsalted butter, softened

3 large eggs

1 cup | 250 mL plus 2 Tbsp | 25 mL granulated sugar

1 Tbsp | 15 mL instant espresso powder

1 Tbsp | 15 mL vanilla extract

6 Tbsp | 90 mL sifted all-purpose flour

3/4 tsp | 4 mL salt

1/2 tsp | 2 mL baking powder

1¹/₂ cups | 375 mL walnuts, toasted

1¹/₂ cups | 375 mL pecans, toasted

Preheat the oven to 325°F | 160°C.

In a double boiler or a metal bowl set over a pan of barely simmering water, melt all the unsweetened chocolate and half (9 oz | 250 g) of the semisweet chocolate with the butter. Stir it occasionally. Remove the top of the double boiler or the bowl from the heat.

In a bowl, beat the eggs and sugar with an electric mixer until they're light and fluffy. Add the espresso powder, vanilla and chocolate mixture, beating the batter until it's smooth.

In a small bowl, whisk together the flour, salt and baking powder. Add this to the chocolate mixture, beating it until just combined. Stir in the remaining semisweet chocolate and nuts until they're well combined.

With an ice-cream scoop, arrange generous measures of cookie dough about 3 inches | 8 cm apart on ungreased baking sheets. Bake the cookies in batches in the middle of the oven for 25 minutes or less (depending on their size), until the tops begin to crack. You don't want to overbake them. Cool the cookies on a rack.

Zoë's parfait

Serves 4 to 6

Here's a simple dessert that my daughter, Zoë, who gets A's in home ec, invented.

2 flavors of ice cream, gelato or sorbet, such as mango and raspberry or banana and coconut

1 cup | 250 mL blueberries

1/2 cup | 125 mL strawberries, sliced in half if large

shredded coconut

zest of one lemon, grated or finely minced

With an ice-cream scoop, place 3 scoops of ice cream, gelato or sorbet for each person being served in individual serving dishes. Zoë recommends that you put them together in a wine or champagne glass for a semi-formal appearance. Tumble blueberries and strawberries over top. Sprinkle coconut and a little lemon zest on each dessert. Voila!

PLANK-baked APPLES with rum-honey sauce

Serves 8

Apples, like other tree fruits, cook up really well on a cedar plank. They're great as a dessert but are also an excellent accompaniment to planked pork or poultry.

For the sauce:

1 cup | 250 mL Appleton Estate dark rum

1 cup | 250 mL liquid honey

1/4 tsp | 1 mL grated nutmeg

1 Tbsp | 15 mL butter

For the apples:

1 plank (cedar or fruitwoods work best), soaked overnight or at least 1 hour

8 firm, ripe cooking apples (Granny Smith, Jonathan, McIntosh, Winesap)

2 Tbsp | 25 mL butter at room temperature

2 Tbsp | 25 mL raisins

2 Tbsp | 25 mL dark brown sugar

1/4 tsp | 1 mL ground ginger

1/4 tsp | 1 mL ground cinnamon

pinch cloves

freshly grated nutmeg

pinch salt

vanilla ice cream (optional)

Combine the rum, honey and nutmeg in a saucepan, taking care not to expose the alcohol to any flame, and bring to a slow boil. Use a fairly deep pan and tend this carefully, because it can boil over. Reduce by about half, or until the mixture is a thick syrup that coats the back of a spoon. Take the pan off the heat and set aside, reserving the butter for finishing the sauce.

Slice the tops off the apples and scoop out the cores, taking care not to cut through the bottom of the apples (a melon baller works great). Mix together the butter, raisins, sugar, spices and salt. Spoon the sugar/butter mixture into the cavities. (I eat whatever can't fit into the apples like the little piggy I am.) Tear some extra-wide foil into 10-inch | 25-cm squares and wrap the foil around the bottoms of the apples, leaving the tops exposed. (This helps cook the apples evenly and also makes it easier to place them securely on the plank.)

Preheat the grill on medium-high for 5 or 10 minutes or until the chamber temperature rises above 500°F | 260°C. Rinse the plank and place it on the cooking grate. Cover the grill and heat the plank for 4 or 5 minutes, or until it starts to throw off a bit of smoke and crackles lightly. Reduce the heat to medium and place the apples carefully on the plank. Cook for about 20 to 25 minutes or until they're tender and the filling is bubbling.

Transfer the apples from the grill to a platter and let them rest for a few minutes. While the apples are resting, warm the sauce and add the butter, stirring until it's incorporated. Serve the apples in a pool of the sauce, with a scoop of ice cream on the side.

PLANKING ❥ SECRETS ❧

Soak your plank in something other than water to create extra aroma. Try apple juice or wine, or add some rum or Jack Daniel's to the soaking water.

Drill eight or ten 1/2-inch | 1-cm holes through your plank before you soak it to create more air flow, and therefore more smoke. If you do this, take extra care to watch for flare-ups.

rum-honey PLANKED PINEAPPLE

Serves 4 to 6

You guessed it: I love rum and honey. The strong flavor of pineapple is nicely enhanced by the aroma of the cedar, and the rum-honey marinade gives this dessert extra richness and complexity.

1 cedar plank, soaked overnight or at least 1 hour

1/2 cup | 125 mL liquid honey

2 Tbsp | 25 mL fresh lime juice

2 Tbsp | 25 mL Appleton Estate dark rum

1 Tbsp | 15 mL lime zest, finely chopped or grated

1 large ripe pineapple

1/4 cup | 50 mL chopped fresh mint

vanilla ice cream (optional)

Mix the honey, lime juice, rum and lime zest together in a nonreactive bowl. Trim the peel off the pineapple and cut it into 6 disks, removing and discarding the core. Add the pineapple to the honey mixture and turn to coat. Cover and marinate for at least 1 hour and up to 2 hours.

Preheat the grill on medium-high for 5 or 10 minutes or until the chamber temperature rises above 500°F | 260°C. Rinse the plank and place it on the cooking grate. Cover the grill and heat the plank for 4 or 5 minutes, or until it starts to throw off a bit of smoke and crackles lightly. Reduce the heat to medium.

Place the pineapple chunks on the plank, reserving the marinade. Cook for about 10 minutes or until the pineapple is hot and just starting to brown around the edges. Serve with vanilla ice cream and use the reserved marinade as a finishing glaze.

PLANKED bananas FOSTER

Serves 4

I remember having Bananas Foster at Brennan's restaurant as part of a brunch that cost my wife and me $90. It was worth it just for the stories our veteran waiter told while he was flambéing the bananas. This planked version of the classic New Orleans dessert gives the bananas a slightly smoky flavor that nicely contrasts with the rich, syrupy sweetness of the sauce.

1 cedar plank, soaked overnight or at least 1 hour

**4 ripe but not overripe bananas,
cut in half lengthwise, then halved**

1/4 cup | 50 mL butter

1 cup | 250 mL brown sugar

1/2 tsp | 2 mL ground cinnamon

1/4 cup | 50 mL banana liqueur

**1/4 cup | 50 mL Appleton Estate dark rum
in a small bowl or ramekin**

4 scoops vanilla ice cream

Preheat the grill on medium-high for 5 or 10 minutes or until the chamber temperature rises above 500°F | 260°C. Rinse the plank and place it on the cooking grate. Cover the grill and heat the plank for 4 or 5 minutes, or until it starts to throw off a bit of smoke and crackles lightly. Reduce the heat to medium.

Put the bananas on the plank, cut side up, and cover the grill. Cook for about 8 to 10 minutes or until they turn light golden and are soft but not mushy. Remove and set aside.

As soon as the bananas are off the plank, combine the butter, sugar and cinnamon in a flambé pan or heavy skillet and heat, stirring, just until the sugar dissolves. Stir in the banana liqueur and transfer the bananas to the skillet. When the mixture is warm, carefully add the rum. If you're cooking on a gas stove, tip the pan slightly to ignite the rum. For an electric stove, use a barbecue lighter or a match to do the same. Serve hot, placing the bananas on a scoop of ice cream and spooning the sauce over top.

PLANKED GRAPEFRUIT with GRAND MARNIER AND HONEY

Serves 8

Trust me! This is delicious. I got the idea from one of the pioneers of plank-cooking, Malcolm York. Malcolm wrote the excellent book *Introduction to Plank Barbecuing,* which includes a planked grapefruit recipe featuring sweet vermouth and cherries.

1 cedar plank, soaked overnight or at least 1 hour

4 pink grapefruits, cut in half

Grand Marnier

1/2 cup | 125 mL liquid honey

vanilla ice cream

Prepare the grapefruits as if you were going to have them for breakfast, making cuts to loosen the segments in the skin. Drizzle each grapefruit with about 1 tsp | 5 mL of the liqueur.

Preheat the grill on medium-high for 5 or 10 minutes or until the chamber temperature rises above 500°F | 260°C. Rinse the plank and place it on the cooking grate. Cover the grill and heat the plank for 4 or 5 minutes, or until it starts to throw off a bit of smoke and crackles lightly.

Place the grapefruit halves, cut side up, on the plank, close the grill and reduce the heat to medium. Cook for about 10 minutes. Remove from the plank, place on dessert plates and drizzle with honey. Place a small scoop of ice cream on top and serve.

PLANKED PEAR crisp

Serves 6 to 8

The late, great essayist Laurie Colwin wrote about food in a way that was funny, homey and totally inviting. My wife Kate has made this pear crisp of Colwin's on many occasions, but one of the most memorable times we have had it was with friends on an early fall evening at Vancouver's Spanish Banks beach. We reheated it in its pan on our portable charcoal grill. The sound of the surf, the lights starting to twinkle on the opposite shore, and warm, crunchy, slightly smoky pear crisp. Bliss. Plank-cooking the crisp is optional. It works well in a good old convection oven, too.

1 fruitwood plank (apple or cherry would work well),
soaked overnight or at least 1 hour

4 lb | 2 kg ripe pears, unpeeled, cut into chunks

1/4 cup | 50 mL granulated sugar, or less

1/4 cup | 50 mL fresh lemon juice

1 sprig of fresh rosemary (optional)

3/4 cup | 175 mL brown sugar

1 cup | 250 mL all-purpose flour

1/2 cup | 125 mL cold butter

rind of 1 lemon

vanilla ice cream (optional)

In a large bowl, toss the pear chunks with the granulated sugar and lemon juice. Pour this mixture into a large baking pan. For a sophisticated touch, place a sprig of rosemary in the bottom of the mixture; if children are going to run away screaming, omit this step.

Rub together the brown sugar, flour and butter. An easy way to achieve the desired texture is to put the butter in the freezer beforehand and then grate it into the other ingredients using a large holed grater. The topping is supposed to be crumbly. Sprinkle it over the pears.

Preheat the grill on medium-high for 5 or 10 minutes or until the chamber temperature rises above 500°F | 260°C. Rinse the plank and place it on the cooking grate. Cover the grill and heat the plank for 4 or 5 minutes, or until it starts to throw off a bit of smoke and crackles lightly.

Reduce the heat to low (you want the chamber temperature to stabilize at about 350 to 400°F | 180 to 200°C) and place the baking dish on top of the plank (if the plank is warping from the heat, turn it upside down and wait a few more minutes until it flattens). Bake until the pears are tender and the topping is golden brown and crunchy, about 1 hour. Cool for 20 minutes before serving. Vanilla ice cream goes nicely.

MISSION HILL **planked** PEACHES WITH rhubarb compote

Serves 8

One of the highlights of my barbecue career so far was a grilling and barbecue class I taught in the summer of 2004 at the beautiful Mission Hill Family Estate in the heart of British Columbia's wine country. My friend, Winery Chef Michael Allemeier, created this dish especially for the occasion. The first time it was served, we used pears because they were in season, but the ideal fruit is perfectly ripe peaches. It takes a little more prep time than most desserts. It also takes a whole 350-mL bottle of icewine, which ain't cheap. But it's worth it to see the look on your guests' faces when they taste this splendid creation.

NOTE: The rhubarb compote makes about 2 quarts/litres, which is more than you need, but it's great stirred with yogurt or spooned onto ice cream, waffles or pancakes.

For the icewine reduction:

3/4 cup | 175 mL icewine (preferably Mission Hill Vidal Icewine or Mission Hill Late Harvest Vidal)

2 Tbsp | 25 mL liquid honey

6 fresh lavender blossoms (or 1 Tbsp | 15 mL dried lavender)

For the rhubarb compote:

2/3 cup | 150 mL water

3/4 cup | 175 mL (the rest of the bottle) icewine

1¼ lb | 625 g sugar

1 vanilla bean, cut in half lengthwise and scraped

2 lemons, juiced and zested

2 lb | 1 kg rhubarb, washed and diced into 1/4-inch | 5-mm pieces

For the honey-whiskey sauce (with acknowledgements to Ted Reader):

3/4 cup | 175 mL Jack Daniel's

1/2 cup | 125 mL honey

freshly ground black pepper

freshly grated nutmeg

For the peaches:

2 cedar planks, soaked overnight or at least 1 hour

4 large ripe freestone peaches or 8 small ripe Bartlett pears

1 Tbsp | 15 mL lemon juice

1 vanilla bean

1 cup | 250 mL whipping cream

1 Tbsp | 15 mL sugar

To make the icewine reduction, combine the ingredients and heat in a saucepan over medium heat. Gently boil until reduced by about half. Strain and cool. This keeps, refrigerated, for several weeks.

To make the rhubarb compote, combine the water, icewine, sugar, vanilla, lemon juice and zest in a pot and bring to a simmer. Remove from the heat and let sit for 10 minutes. Strain through a fine sieve. Add the rhubarb, bring to a low boil and simmer for about 20 minutes, or until the fruit is very soft and begins to fall apart. Remove from the heat and let cool. Keeps in the fridge for several weeks or indefinitely if you preserve it, hot, in sterilized jars.

To make the honey-whisky sauce, combine the ingredients and heat in a saucepan over medium heat. (Please be very careful with whisky on the stove. Pour it away from the flame and never let the mixture boil over.) Gently boil until the sauce is reduced by half and coats the back of a spoon. Set aside.

Cut the peaches in half, remove the pits, and carefully pare off the peels. (If using pears, slice them in half lengthwise and core them with a melon baller or teaspoon. Make about 5 or 6 slices 1/4 inch | 5 mm thick along the length of the pears, starting each slice just below the stem, so that you can fan them out like a deck of cards and still keep each half intact.) Place the trimmed fruit in a nonreactive dish just large enough to hold them and brush them with lemon juice. Spoon about 1 tsp | 5 mL of honey-whisky sauce over each piece of fruit. Let them marinate for about an hour.

Split the vanilla bean lengthwise and scrape the seeds into a chilled bowl. Whip the cream with the vanilla seeds and sugar until it forms soft peaks.

Preheat the grill on medium-high for 5 or 10 minutes or until the chamber temperature rises above 500°F | 260°C. Rinse the plank and place it on the cooking grate. Cover the grill and heat the plank for 4 or 5 minutes, or until it starts to throw off a bit of smoke and crackles lightly. Reduce the heat to medium. Carefully place the fruit pieces on the plank. Cook for 10 to 12 minutes until tender. (Peaches will char a little around the edges, and pears will turn golden).

Present the fruit in a pool of the rhubarb compote. Add a dollop of whipped cream topped with the whisky sauce, and drizzle the icewine reduction around the edge of the plate. If you want to be truly decadent, serve this with another bottle of the icewine.

PLANKED PEARS WITH walnuts and blue cheese

Serves 8

This is a classic flavor combination, adapted for the plank. Serve these with a scoop of vanilla ice cream and/or a glass of the fortified wine you used to top off the pears.

1 cedar plank, soaked overnight or at least 1 hour

1/2 cup | 125 mL walnuts

4 large ripe pears, peeled and halved, with the cores scooped out

1/4 cup | 50 mL dark brown sugar

1/2 cup | 125 mL crumbled blue cheese

port or sherry

vanilla ice cream (optional)

In a 400°F | 200°C oven, toast the walnuts on a baking sheet for about 10 minutes or until they start to darken and produce a nice aroma. Remove from the oven and cool slightly. Coarsely chop them and set aside. Place the pears, cut side up, on a baking sheet. (If they don't balance well, slice a bit from the bottom to make them sit evenly.) Sprinkle them with the brown sugar and put about 1 Tbsp | 15 mL of cheese in the depression of each pear. Top each off with just a touch of port or sherry.

Preheat the grill on medium-high for 5 or 10 minutes or until the chamber temperature rises above 500°F | 260°C. Rinse the plank and place it on the cooking grate. Cover the grill and heat the plank for 4 or 5 minutes, or until it starts to throw off a bit of smoke and crackles lightly. Reduce the heat to medium-low.

Place the pears on the plank, taking care not to tip them, and cook for 10 minutes or until the cheese is melted and the pears are golden and tender. Remove from the plank, sprinkle some chopped walnuts over each pear and serve immediately.

RAISE A GLASS TO WOOD
Great Summer Cocktails

Chapter 8

I love to drink. There, I said it. Now I'd like to back up that statement with a few great drink recipes that seem designed to go well with planking, or backyard cooking, or just eating and living in general.

SHAKEN JAMAICAN

Serves 1

One of the dreams of anyone who aspires to live the barbecue lifestyle is to make friends with a liquor rep. I achieved this career milestone in the past year, and I'm delighted to know Chris Brown, who among other things represents Appleton Estate Jamaica Rum. Through Chris, Appleton sponsors the Canadian National Barbecue Championships in Whistler, British Columbia. He's a great supporter of championship barbecue, but he also pours a mean summer cocktail. Whether it's winter or summer, you can bring on some Jamaican sunshine with this delicious drink.

1$\frac{1}{2}$ oz Appleton Estate VX

1 oz cherry brandy

3 oz pineapple juice

3 oz orange juice

Shake with ice and strain into martini glass.

DIRTY BANANA

Serves 1

This rum-based drink, also from my friend Chris Brown, makes any time, or day, or location, a tropical celebration.

1$\frac{1}{2}$ oz Appleton Estate VX

1/2 oz Sangster's Jamaica Rum Cream

2 oz pineapple juice

2 oz orange juice

**quarter of a banana
(half if you really like banana)**

Blend until smooth. Serve in a hurricane glass. Garnish with fresh fruit.

THE D.J. SMOOTHIE

Serves 2

My son Jake is the pickiest eater on the planet —not easy for parents who want him to eat something other than chicken nuggets and plain cheese pizza. But his sensitive palate is going to serve him well one day as a chef or sommelier. It's already starting to pay dividends. Watching me experiment with planking recipes, he decided he was going to develop some blender drinks. So far his favorite is a Smore Smoothy, consisting of chocolate sauce, ice cream and graham crackers—a bit sweet for some tastes. The following tangy treat, however, has wide appeal, and with a little rum might even make it on the cocktail circuit. (The D.J. Smoothie is named after Jake and his friend David, who co-developed the recipe and helped mess-up the kitchen in the process.)

2 ice cubes

2 lemons

2 limes

2 oranges

1 banana

1 pinch sugar (optional)

3 decent-sized chunks watermelon

3 decent-sized chunks cantaloupe

small handful blueberries

Whiz together in a blender and serve. Then turn the house into a junk-heap or play some video games.

NU'S DANUBE

Serves 1

My wife, Kate, got a gig that most men would dream of—she's the new booze columnist for a big daily newspaper. She gets to go and taste drinks and talk to club owners, bartenders and liquor experts about drinks, and then write about it. In her travels she runs into great cocktail recipes. This recipe was invented by Jay Jones of Nu, a trendy Vancouver bar.

1 oz vodka

1/2 oz Grand Marnier

1/2 oz raspberry liqueur

1/4 lime, cut into segments

a dozen blueberries

In a shaker, "muddle" the mixture together with a pestle until the juice has been extracted from the limes and the blueberries are puréed. Add ice up to the rim of the shaker, close it and shake it enough to chill it, about 15 seconds. Strain the drink and serve it in a martini glass.

SUZETTE

Serves 1

This drink, also by Jay Jones of Nu, combines some of the classic flavors of French cooking in a delicious cocktail.

**1½ oz Navan Vanilla
(a vanilla-infused cognac)**

1/2 oz Grand Marnier Cordon Rouge

1 oz freshly squeezed lime juice

dash of orange-flavored bitters

freshly shaved orange and lime rind (optional)

Pour these ingredients over ice in a shaker, close the shaker, shake about 15 seconds and strain. Serve in a martini glass, garnished with the citrus rinds.

GEORGE'S HONEY MULE

Serves 1

This is a recipe from bartender Nick Devine at Vancouver's George Ultra Lounge. It's based on the recipe for a Moscow Mule, but it packs even more of a kick!

1 tsp | 15 mL liquid honey

1½ to 3 oz vodka

squeeze fresh lime

dash Angostura bitters

ginger beer

Pour the honey into the bottom of a cocktail glass and add one or two shots of vodka, to taste. Mix together slowly and thoroughly, until the honey has dissolved. Then, and only then, add ice, a squeeze of fresh lime juice and a dash of Angostura bitters. Top the lot with ginger beer.

WHITE PORT AND TONIC

Manuel Ferreira, owner of two excellent restaurants in Vancouver, Le Gavroche and Senova, says this is a favorite drink in his home country, Portugal. It goes well with salted nuts.

3 oz Taylor Fladgate white port

9 oz tonic water

basil sprig

Pour the port into a tall glass with ice cubes. Top it with the tonic. Garnish with the basil sprig and serve.

PLANK-COOKED MENUS FOR ANY OCCASION

Scallop and Cucumber Salad   68

Cedar-Planked Salmon with
Whiskey-Maple Glaze   103

Florida Grilled Zucchini   92

Roasted Garlic Mashed Potatoes   96

Mission Hill Planked Peaches
with Rhubarb Compote   192

Plank-Roasted Red Pepper Soup   61

Cumin-Curry Basa
with Banana-Yogurt Salsa   127

Grilled Asparagus   90

Cuban-Style Black Beans   98

Planked Bananas Foster   189

Lime-Ginger Risotto   99

Asian Lamb Racks   176

Asian Slaw   82

Wasabi Mashed Potatoes   97

Planked Grapefruit with
Grand Marnier and Honey   190

Salmon Cakes (appetizer portion)   100

Harvest Time Pork Tenderloin   168

Plank-Baked Apples with
Rum-Honey Sauce   186

Maple-Planked Butternut
Squash Purée   75

Allan's Chile Corn Cakes   94

Zoë's Parfait   185

The Baron's Planked Sweet
Hickory Bacon Bites   60

Planked Rack of Venison
with Balsamic Raspberry Glaze   172

Stuffed Mushrooms   54

Rosemary Roasted Carrots   91

Planked Pear Crisp   191

Kickin' Crab Salad   88

Fred's Citrus Salmon   112

Wilted Summer Lettuce Salad   89

Pauline's Wild Rice Salad   84

Black and Blue Berries
with Lime Zest Confit   181

Planked Asparagus and
Prosciutto Bundles   67

Salmon with Pesto   113

Fettuccini Alfredo   93

Planked Pears with
Walnuts and Blue Cheese   194

MUSIC TO PLANK BY

In my first cookbook, *Barbecue Secrets*, I devoted a page to the music that I like to barbecue by. Since then, I've further refined my tastes and also focused on a specific genre, country rock, which seems to go really well with backyard cooking. In my quest for the perfect country rock playlist, here's what I've come up with. I invite you to write me at rockinronnie@ronshewchuk.com if you have any suggestions for expanding or improving this collection of songs. In the meantime, visit iTunes, download to your heart's content and rock on!

NAME	ARTIST
Come On (Single)	Chuck Berry & Martha Berry
Sweet City Woman	Stampeders
Uncle John's Band	Grateful Dead
Hot Rod Lincoln	Commander Cody & His Lost Planet Airmen
Rocket	Kathy Mattea
Waiting for the Sun	The Jayhawks
Ramblin' Man	The Allman Brothers Band
Dixie Chicken	Little Feat
Sweet Home Alabama	Lynyrd Skynrd
La Grange	ZZ Top
Free Bird	Lynyrd Skynrd
Mississippi Queen	Mountain
Jesus Is Just Alright	The Doobie Brothers
It's a Great Day to Be Alive	Travis Tritt
Hurt	Johnny Cash
Sweet Virginia	The Rolling Stones
Windfall	Son Volt
It'll Shine When It Shines	The Ozark Mountain Daredevils

INDEX

ACKNOWLEDGEMENTS

The platform of this book has been built with the planks of many supporters and contributors, starting with the good folks at Williams Sonoma, who saw the need for this book and who had the faith to put in a big advance order. I'm forever grateful for your patronage and excellent merchandizing skills.

My wife gets second billing (as usual, she might add) for putting up with all the messes in the kitchen and the endless moaning about how much work a cookbook takes to write—not to mention her new batch of exceptional dessert recipes and her excellent editing and proofreading. Another key source of support, always there for me in my darkest hours, is my agent and friend Robert Mackwood.

Then there are my good friends at Westcoast Lifestyles, who manufacture the best cooking planks on the planet and who contributed stacks of their product in support of this book's development.

For me, cooking is much more than a technical chore. It's a spiritual quest, a continuing journey of discovery that allows us to understand who we are and what's important in the world. Special thanks go to Chef Bev Antoine, sous-chef Raymond Johnston, Kathy Parkinson and the rest of the team at the Quw'utsun' Cultural Centre for educating me in the history and techniques of aboriginal cooking.

But more than anything, it's the many contributors to this book who made it possible, from old and new friends like Michelle Allaire, Carolyn Rowan, Jenny Neidhart, Margie Gibb, Amo Jackson, Mike Dos Santos, Christine Hunt, Bryan O'Connor, Chris Brown, Pauline Bahnsen, Kim Peterson, Diane Read, Gail Norton, Terry and Cathy Kelly, Lawrence Davis, Brian Misko, Fred Kraus, Stuart Parker, Reza Mofakham and some of the icons and demi-gods of outdoor (and indoor) cooking, including my dear brother, Allan Shewchuk, Bob Lyon, Ted Reader, Nathan Fong, Hidekazu Tojo, Stephen Raichlen, Paul Kirk, Cheryl and Bill Jamison, John Howie, Michael Allemeier and the late, great David Veljacic, the one and only Fire Chef. Thank you for your generous contributions to this book. If variety is the spice of life, you've helped me put together a jambalaya of a book!

And, finally, a big thank you to all the folks who helped produce this book: food stylist Nathan Fong and photographer Greg Athans, designers Jacqui Thomas and Five Seventeen, editor Elaine Jones and the rest of the great team at Whitecap Books, including Michael Burch, Robert McCullough, AnnMarie MacKinnon, Alicia Schlag, Brian Forbes, Aydin Virani and Mark MacDonald.

Thank you all, from the charred bottom of my heart!

PLANKING RESOURCES

These days you can find cooking planks at most gourmet food stores, barbecue specialty stores, home improvement centers, hardware stores and big supermarkets. If you can't find planks in your neighborhood, visit these websites to find good quality mail-order planks.

www.westcoastlifestyles.com
www.plankcooking.com
www.barbecuewood.com

For hard-to-find mesquite planks, order by telephone from Rancho Lobos in Mexico at 520-225-0415.